# Career **SUCCESS**

### Third Edition

## Marsha Fralick

Cover image © Shutterstock, Inc.

**Kendall Hunt**
publishing company

www.kendallhunt.com
*Send all inquiries to*:
4050 Westmark Drive
Dubuque, IA 52004-1840

Copyright © 2014, 2018, 2021 by Kendall Hunt Publishing Company

PAK ISBN 978-1-7924-6698-4
Text alone ISBN 978-1-7924-6699-1

Published in the United States of America

# BRIEF CONTENTS

# CONTENTS

# 5 Planning Your Career and Education   139

# 6 Updated Job Search Strategies   171

# 7 Career Satisfaction   205

## Index   245

# PREFACE

Among the most important decisions a person will make in life are, "What is my major?" and "What is my ideal career?" I have observed that students choose their careers for a variety of reasons. Some students choose a career based on a person they admire. Maybe they have experienced a nurse who was helpful or a veterinarian that took care of a pet and based their career decisions on this personal experience. Some choose their career based on familiarity. They choose occupations that they have observed in their families or communities. Others choose a career by accident; they obtain whatever job is available. This can result in dissatisfaction and a dislike of work if the occupation is not a good match with personal strengths and interests. We now have a great deal of information on how to choose a satisfying career goal. The first step is personal assessment. What are the students' personality types, interests, skills, and values? Once these are determined, what careers match these personal characteristics?

Knowing your personal strengths and skills will help you to find your passion so that you can find personal fulfillment in the career you choose. The famous painter, Picasso, found work to be relaxing and said that time flies when you have found your passion. One of the famous quotes by author Mark Twain was, "The secret of success is making your vocation your vacation." He added that if you do this, you never have to work a day in your life. When we find careers that match our personalities and personal strengths, we provide meaning and interest to our lives.

Over the years I have asked students to state why they are going to college and they frequently state that their goal is to be happy. However, if they do not have a clear idea of what happiness means, they may not reach their goal. Sometimes we define happiness by the things in our lives: our homes, cars, and money for vacations and other goods. Psychologist Martin Seligman, author of *Authentic Happiness*, has found that true happiness exists when you have found your passion and experience the state of "flow," when you are completely absorbed in an activity that matches your personal strengths. When you are in this state of flow, you are happier and more productive. You don't have to spend the work week looking forward to Fridays.

The greatest disappointment for a college student is to graduate from college and be unable to find a job in their chosen career. Today it is important to take a look at the job outlook and match your personal strengths to jobs that are available and pay enough for you to live your preferred lifestyle. To assure that you can find your preferred career after graduation, it is important to start the career planning process early. Determine your strengths, examine the job outlook, and prepare for your career, starting at the beginning of college rather than waiting until after graduation. It is also important to be able to use updated job search strategies to find your job. Establish your personal brand online and use new media and social networking to find a job.

Although it is unrealistic that you will enjoy every day at work or like all your work, it is good to enjoy your work at least most of the time. It is not good to hate Mondays. This textbook helps you to think about how you can be satisfied with your career. The last step is setting some meaningful career goals for the future and to begin taking action to achieve them.

After over 50 years in education, my greatest satisfaction is helping students to discover their personal strengths, interests, skills, and values and to use this knowledge to find happiness in careers that provide personal fulfillment. This is my motivation for writing *Career Success*. I hope you find it helpful.

# ACKNOWLEDGMENTS

I would like to give my sincere thanks to:

- My parents, Clarence and Betty Finley, who taught me the value of education.
- My seven brothers and sisters who taught me to laugh at life.
- My children, Mark Fralick and Sara Corbett, who challenge me to keep up to date with technology.
- Chelsea Fralick, who provided content editing for the new material in this textbook.
- Paul Delys, who provided love and encouragement and shared many of his ideas and materials for this book.
- The many instructors who tried out my materials, gave valuable feedback, and shared their ideas.
- The many students who have taken my courses over the years and shared their insights and experiences with me.

# ABOUT THE AUTHOR

Dr. Marsha Fralick has been employed in the field of education for over 50 years, including 43 years teaching college and career success courses. She has brought together theories from counseling, positive psychology, and career development to provide students with strategies for career success. Her College and Career Success Program at Cuyamaca College in El Cajon, California, is recognized as an exemplary program by students and statewide organizations. In 2011 she received recognition for her lifetime of achievement by receiving an award for Outstanding First-Year Student Advocate sponsored by the National Resource Center for the First-Year Experience and Students in Transition from the University of South Carolina. Her college and career success materials are now used by community colleges and universities nationwide. She has a doctorate from the University of Southern California in higher education with an emphasis in career counseling, a master's degree in counseling from the University of Redlands, and a bachelor's degree in Spanish and English from Arizona State University. She currently resides in San Diego, California.

Used with permission. © Shutterfly, LLC.

# Create Your Success

# 1

Read to answer these key questions:

- What is my personal definition of career success?

- What are the steps in choosing a major and planning a career?

- How does education affect my future earnings?

- How can I motivate myself to be successful?

- How can I increase my positive thinking about the future?

- How can I take control of my life and create the future I want?

- How do beliefs affect my future success?

- What are some secrets to happiness?

- What does happiness mean to me?

Most students go to college to find happiness, fulfillment, and a satisfying career. The first step is choosing a major and finding the career that matches your personal strengths, interests, and values. One of the keys to success is the belief that you can create your success and then take the steps to make it happen. In this chapter you will explore motivational techniques for increasing your success and some tools for creating the future you want. Finally, you will give some thought to what happiness means to you.

## What Is Career Success?

Career success is much more than accomplishments such as degrees, job titles, and high pay. As a beginning step in achieving career success, take some time to think about your personal definition of success.

As you think about the meaning of career success, consider these elements:

- doing what you enjoy
- feeling happy and fulfilled in your life
- earning at least enough money for the necessities of life and financial self-sufficiency
- using grit and perseverance to overcome obstacles in life and careers
- thinking positively and practicing a growth mindset
- being motivated to accomplish your goals
- realizing that you create your success
- taking care of your physical and mental health

This chapter explores many of the topics listed above and provides the opportunity to reflect on your personal meaning of career success.

# Choosing Your Major and Finding Your Ideal Career

Choosing your major is one of the most important decisions you will make in college, because it will have a big impact on your future career. It is difficult to motivate yourself and put in the work necessary to be successful if you do not have a clear picture of your future career. How do people choose a major and then find their ideal career? This course will help you to become aware of the steps needed to think critically about yourself and the world of work to make a good career decision. Here are the steps in choosing your major and finding that ideal career:

- **Realize that you can create your own future.** Chapter 1 provides some tools for creating your future, including motivation, thinking positively, understanding locus of control, optimism, belief in yourself, visualizing your success, and thinking about what it really means to be happy in your life.
- **Assess your personality type.** The TruTalent Personality assessment in Chapter 2 will help you to identify your personal strengths and matching careers. It will also give you some information about what is required for career satisfaction.
- **Explore your vocational interests and values.** The Interest Profiler integrated into Chapter 3 will help you to explore your vocational interests. Exercises within this chapter will help clarify your values, or what is most important in your life. Making a career decision based on your personal values will enable to you to find work that you find important.
- **Discover your multiple intelligences.** In Chapter 4, you will learn about the many ways people are intelligent and how to improve your skills by exploring your mindset and grit. This chapter includes the TruTalent Intelligences assessment to learn about your multiple intelligences and matching careers.
- **Learn about the job market.** Learn about career trends and opportunities in Chapter 5 and how you can match your personal strengths to the job market. This chapter includes the TruTalent Skills assessment and matches your skills to careers and actual job openings.
- **Gain job skills while in college.** Chapter 6 begins with some ways to increase your prospects of finding meaningful employment after college by using career services, volunteering, doing internships, and working part time.
- **Use updated job search strategies.** Chapter 6 continues with some ideas for using new media, which has provided many opportunities for marketing your personal brand and using online tools to locate your ideal job.
- **Plan a satisfying career.** Chapter 7 helps you to understand the factors related to career satisfaction and how to be successful on the job.

## Journal
## Entry

Write a paragraph about deciding on your ideal major and career. Use any of these questions to guide your thinking: If you have chosen a major, why is it the best major for you? Does this major help you to live your preferred lifestyle? If you have not chosen a major, what are some steps in choosing the right major and career? What qualities would you look for in an ideal career? What is your preferred lifestyle?

"The purpose of our lives is to give birth to the best which is within us."

MARIANNE WILLIAMSON

© IQONCEPT/SHUTTERSTOCK.COM

## Using Motivation to Increase Your Success

### What Is the Value of a College Education?

Many college students say that getting a satisfying job that pays well and achieving financial security are important motivators for attending college. As a result of the rising cost of higher education, students have started to question whether a college education is still a good investment. Recent analyses by the Federal Reserve Bank have shown that the benefits still outweigh the cost for both an associate's and a bachelor's degree. These degrees have a 15% return, which is considered a good investment.[1] By getting a degree, you can get a job that pays more per hour, work fewer hours to earn a living, and have more time for leisure activities. In addition, you can spend your time at work doing something that you enjoy. A report issued by the US Bureau of Labor Statistics in 2020 listed the following education and income statistics for all races and both genders throughout the United States.[2] Lifetime income assumes that a person works 30 years before retirement.

## Average Earnings Based on Education Level

| Education | Yearly Income | Lifetime Income |
|---|---|---|
| High school graduate | 38,792 | 1,163,760 |
| Some college, no degree | 43,316 | 1,299,480 |
| Associate degree | 46,124 | 1,383,720 |
| Bachelor's degree | 64,896 | 1,946,880 |
| Professional degree | 96,772 | 2,903,160 |

© SERGIGN/SHUTTERSTOCK.COM

Notice that income rises with educational level. Over a lifetime, a person with a bachelor's degree earns about 60% more than a high school graduate. Of course, these are average figures across the nation and some individuals earn higher or lower salaries. People fantasize about winning the lottery, but the reality is that the probability of winning the lottery is very low. In the long run, you have a better chance of increasing your income by going to college.

Let's do some further comparisons. A high-school graduate earns an average of $1,163,760 over a lifetime. A college graduate with a bachelor's degree earns $1,946,880 over a lifetime. A college graduate earns $783,120 more than a high-school graduate does over a lifetime. So how much is a college degree worth? It is worth $783,120 over a lifetime. Would you go to college and finish your degree if someone offered to pay you $783,120? Here are some more interesting figures we can derive from the above table:

Completing one college course is worth $19,578.
($783,120 divided by 40 courses in a bachelor's degree)

Going to class for one hour is worth $408.
($19,578 divided by 48 hours in a semester class)

Would you take a college course if someone offered you $19,578? Would you go to class today for one hour if someone offered you $408? Of course, if this sounds too good to be true, remember that you will receive these payments over a working lifetime of 30 years.

While college graduation does not guarantee employment, it increases your chances of finding a job. College graduates have lower unemployment rates as compared to high school graduates. Increase your chances of finding employment by continuing your education.

Employment and earnings are only some of the values of going to college. College helps develop your potential and increase your confidence, self-esteem, self-respect, and happiness. It increases your understanding of the world and prepares you to be an informed citizen.

## Journal Entry

What are your dreams for the future? Write a paragraph about what you hope to accomplish by going to college.

**2**

## Intrinsic or Extrinsic Motivation

**Intrinsic motivation** comes from within. It means that you do an activity because you enjoy it or find personal meaning in it. With intrinsic motivation, the nature of the activity itself or the consequences of the activity motivate you. For example, let's say that I am interested in learning to play the piano. I am motivated to practice playing the piano, because I like the sound of the piano and feel very satisfied when I can play music that I enjoy. I practice because I like to practice, not because I have to practice. When I get tired or frustrated, I work through it or put it aside and come back to it, because I want to learn to play the piano well.

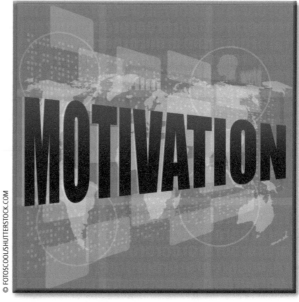

© FOTOSCOOL/SHUTTERSTOCK.COM

You can be intrinsically motivated to continue in college and achieve your career goals, because you enjoy learning and find the college experience satisfying. Look for ways to enjoy college and to find some personal satisfaction in it. If you enjoy college, it becomes easier to do the work required to be successful. Think about what you say to yourself about college. If you are saying negative things such as, "I don't want to be here," it will be difficult to continue.

**Extrinsic motivation** comes as a result of an external reward from someone else. Examples of extrinsic rewards are certificates, bonuses, money, praise, and recognition. Taking the piano example again, let's say that I want my child to play the piano. The child does not know if he or she would like to play the piano. I give the child a reward for practicing the piano. I could pay the child for practicing or give praise for doing a good job. There are two possible outcomes of the extrinsic reward. After a while, the child may gain skills and confidence and come to enjoy playing the piano. The extrinsic reward is no longer necessary, because the child is now intrinsically motivated. Or the child may decide that he or she does not like to play the piano. The extrinsic reward is no longer effective in motivating the child to play the piano.

You can use extrinsic rewards to motivate yourself to be successful in college. Remind yourself of the payoff for getting a college degree: earning more money, having a satisfying career, being able to purchase a car and a house. Extrinsic rewards can be a first step in motivating yourself to attend college. With experience and achievement, you may come to like going to college and may become intrinsically motivated to continue your college education.

If you use intrinsic motivation to achieve your goal, you will be happier and more successful. If you do something like playing the piano because you enjoy it, you are more likely to spend the time necessary to practice to achieve your goal. If you view college as something that you enjoy and is valuable to you, it is easier to spend the time to do the required studying. When you get tired or frustrated, tell yourself that you are doing a good job (praise yourself) and think of the positive reasons that you want to get a college education.

> "Ability is what you're capable of doing. Motivation determines what you do. Attitude determines how well you do it."
> RAYMOND CHANDLER

## Thinking Positively about the Future

You can motivate yourself to complete your education by thinking positively about the future. If you believe that your chances of graduating from college are good, you can be motivated to take the steps necessary to achieve your goals. Conversely, if you think that your chances of graduating are poor, it is difficult to motivate yourself to continue. The degree of optimism that you possess is greatly influenced by past experiences. For example, if you were a good student in the past, you are likely to be optimistic about the future. If you struggled with your education, you may have some negative experiences that you will need to overcome. Negative thoughts can often become a self-fulfilling prophecy; what we think becomes true.

How can you train yourself to think more optimistically? First, become aware of your thought patterns. Are they mostly negative or positive? If they are negative, rewind the tape and make them more positive. Here is an example.

### Pessimism

I failed the test. I guess I am just not college material. I feel really stupid. I just can't do this. College is too hard for me. My (teacher, father, mother, friend, boss) told me I would never make it. Maybe I should just drop out of college and do something else.

### Optimism

I failed the test. Let's take a look at what went wrong, so I can do better next time. Did I study enough? Did I study the right material? Maybe I should take this a little slower. How can I get help so that I can understand? I plan to do better next time.

Can a person be too optimistic? In some circumstances, this is true. There is a difference between optimism and wishful thinking, for example. Wishful thinking does not include plans for accomplishing goals and can be a distraction from achieving them. Working toward unattainable goals can be exhausting and demoralizing, especially when the resources for attaining them are lacking. Goals must be realistic and achievable. Psychologists recommend that "people should be optimistic when the future can be changed by positive thinking, but not otherwise."[3] Using optimism requires some judgment about possible outcomes in the future.

There are some good reasons to think more positively. Psychologists have long-term studies showing that people who use positive thinking have many benefits over a lifetime, including good health, longevity, happiness, perseverance, improved problem solving, and enhanced ability to learn. Optimism is also related to goal achievement. If you are optimistic and believe a goal is achievable, you are more likely to take the steps necessary to accomplish the goal. If you do not believe that a goal is achievable, you are likely to give up trying to achieve it.

Being optimistic is closely related to being hopeful about the future. If you are hopeful about the future, you are likely to be more determined to reach your goals and to make plans for reaching them. One research study showed that for entering college freshmen, the level of hope was a better predictor of college grades than standardized tests or high school grade point average.[4] Students with a high level of hope set higher goals and worked to attain those goals. Hopeful people think positively and believe that the future will be good. They change goals and plans when necessary. People who are not hopeful about the future are less likely to be successful. Be optimistic about graduating from college, find the resources necessary to accomplish your goal and start taking the steps to create your success.

# Activity

Are you generally an optimist or pessimist about the future? Read the following items and rate your level of agreement or disagreement.

Rate the following items using this scale:

**5** I definitely agree
**4** I agree
**3** I neither agree or disagree (neutral)
**2** I disagree
**1** I strongly disagree

_____ My chances of graduating from college are good.

_____ I am confident that I can overcome any obstacles to my success.

_____ Things generally turn out well for me.

_____ I believe that positive results will eventually come from most problem situations.

_____ If I work hard enough, I will eventually achieve my goals.

_____ Although I have faced some problems in the past, the future will be better.

_____ I expect that most things will go as planned.

_____ Good things will happen to me in the future.

_____ I am generally persistent in reaching my goals.

_____ I am good at finding solutions to the problems I face in life.

Add up your total points and multiply by two. My total points (X2) are _____.

| | |
|---|---|
| 90–100 | You are an excellent positive thinker. |
| 80–89 | You are a good positive thinker. |
| 70–79 | Sometimes you think positively and sometimes not. Can you re-evaluate your thinking? |
| 60 and below | Work on positive thinking. |

## Journal Entry

Write five positive statements about your college education and future career.

**3**

## Quiz

### Motivation

1. Over a lifetime a college graduate earns about _____ more than a high school graduate.

   a. $250,000
   b. $785,000
   c. $1,000,000

2. As compared to high school graduates, college graduates are

   a. more likely to be unemployed.
   b. less likely to be unemployed.
   c. guaranteed employment.

3. To be successful in college, it is best to use

   a. an external locus of control.
   b. extrinsic motivation.
   c. intrinsic motivation.

4. Intrinsic motivation

   a. comes from within.
   b. is the result of an external reward.
   c. involves higher pay or recognition for a job well done.

5. To increase your chance of accomplishing your goals,

   a. think positively and work step by step to achieve your goals.
   b. use wishful thinking.
   c. set high goals that may not be possible to achieve.

**How did you do on the quiz? Check your answers: 1. b, 2. b, 3. c, 4. a, 5. a**

## Taking Control of Your Life

### Locus of Control

Being aware of the concept of locus of control can help you take control of your life. The word **locus** means place. Locus of control is where you place the responsibility for control over your life. In other words, who is in charge? If you place the responsibility on yourself and believe that you have control over your life, you have internal locus of control. If you place the responsibility on others and think that luck or fate determines your future, you have external locus of control. Some people use internal or external locus of control in combination or favor one type in certain situations. If you favor an internal locus of control, you believe that to a great extent your actions determine your future. Studies have shown that students who use an internal locus of control are likely to have higher achievement in college.[5] The characteristics of students with internal and external locus of control are listed below.

Students with an internal locus of control:

- Believe that they are in control of their lives.
- Understand that grades are directly related to the amount of study invested.

> "I am a great believer in luck and I find that the harder I work, the more I have of it."
>
> THOMAS JEFFERSON

- Are self-motivated.
- Learn from their mistakes by figuring out what went wrong and how to fix the problem.
- Think positively and try to make the best of each situation.
- Rely on themselves to find something interesting in the class and learn the material.

Students with an external locus of control:

- Believe that their lives are largely a result of luck, fate, or chance.
- Think that teachers give grades rather than students earn grades.
- Rely on external motivation from teachers or others.
- Look for someone to blame when they make a mistake.
- Think negatively and believe they are victims of circumstance.
- Rely on the teacher to make the class interesting and to teach the material.

> "Ability is what you're capable of doing.
>
> Motivation determines what you do.
>
> Attitude determines how well you do it."
>
> LOU HOLTZ

© ANSON0618/SHUTTERSTOCK.COM

# Activity

## Internal or External Locus of Control

Decide whether the statement represents an internal or external locus of control and put a checkmark in the appropriate column.

Internal    External

_____  _____   **1.** Much of what happens to us is due to fate, chance, or luck.

_____  _____   **2.** Grades depend on how much work you put into them.

_____  _____   **3.** If I do badly on the test, it is usually because the teacher is unfair.

_____  _____   **4.** If I do badly on the test, it is because I didn't study or didn't understand the material.

_____  _____   **5.** I often get blamed for things that are not my fault.

_____  _____   **6.** I try to make the best of the situation.

_____  _____    **7.** It is impossible to get a good grade if you have a bad instructor.

_____  _____    **8.** I can be successful through hard work.

_____  _____    **9.** If the teacher is not there telling me what to do, I have a hard time doing my work.

_____  _____    **10.** I can motivate myself to study.

_____  _____    **11.** If the teacher is boring, I probably won't do well in class.

_____  _____    **12.** I can find something interesting about each class.

_____  _____    **13.** When bad things are going to happen, there is not much you can do about it.

_____  _____    **14.** I create my own destiny.

_____  _____    **15.** Teachers should motivate the students to study.

_____  _____    **16.** I have a lot of choice about what happens in my life.

As you probably noticed, the even-numbered statements represent internal locus of control. The odd-numbered statements represent external locus of control. Remember that students with an internal locus of control have a greater chance of success in college. It is important to see yourself as responsible for your own success and achievement and to believe that with effort you can achieve your goals.

## Successful Beliefs

Stephen Covey's book, *The 7 Habits of Highly Successful People*, has been described as one of the most influential books of the 20th century.[6] In 2004 he released a new book called *The 8th Habit: From Effectiveness to Greatness.*[7] Your beliefs have a big impact on your success. Use these ideas to take control of your life and improve your chances for success.

1.  **Be proactive.**  Being proactive means accepting responsibility for your life. Covey uses the word "response-ability" for the ability to choose responses. The quality of your life is based on the decisions and responses that you make. Proactive people make things happen through responsibility and initiative. They do not blame circumstances or conditions for their behavior.

2.  **Begin with the end in mind.**  Know what is important and what you wish to accomplish in your life. To be able to do this, you will need to know your values and goals in life. You will need a clear vision of what you want your life to be and where you are headed.

3.  **Put first things first.**  Once you have established your goals and vision for the future, you will need to manage yourself to do what is important first. Set priorities so that you can accomplish the tasks that are important to you.

4. **Think win-win.** In human interactions, seek solutions that benefit everyone. Focus on cooperation rather than competition. If everyone feels good about the decision, there is cooperation and harmony. If one person wins and the other loses, the loser becomes angry and resentful.

5. **First seek to understand, then to be understood.** Too often in our personal communications, we try to talk first and listen later. Often we don't really listen; we use this time to think of our reply. It is best to listen and understand before speaking. Effective communication is one of the most important skills in life.

6. **Synergize.** A simple definition of synergy is that the whole is greater than the sum of its parts. If people can cooperate and have good communication, they can work together as a team to accomplish more than each individual could do separately. Synergy is also part of the creative process.

7. **Sharpen the saw.** Covey shares the story of a man who was trying to cut down a tree with a dull saw. As he struggled to cut the tree, someone suggested that he stop and sharpen the saw. The man said that he did not have time to sharpen the saw, so he continued to struggle. Covey suggests that we need to take time to stop and sharpen the saw. We need to stop working and invest some time in ourselves by staying healthy physically, mentally, spiritually, and socially. We need to take time for self-renewal.

8. **Find your voice and inspire others to find theirs.** Believe that you can make a positive difference in the world and inspire others to do the same. Covey says that leaders "deal with people in a way that will communicate to them their worth and potential so clearly that they will come to see it in themselves." Accomplishing this ideal begins with developing one's own voice or "unique personal significance."[8]

**Successful Beliefs**

- Be proactive
- Begin with the end in mind
- Put first things first
- Think win-win
- First seek to understand, then to be understood
- Synergize
- Sharpen the saw
- Find your voice and inspire others to find theirs

Anthony Robbins defines belief as "any guiding principle, dictum, faith, or passion that can provide meaning and direction in life. . . . Beliefs are the compass and maps that guide us toward our goals and give us the surety to know we'll get there."[9] The beliefs that we have about ourselves determine how much of our potential we will use and how successful we will be in the future. If we have positive beliefs about ourselves, we will feel confident and accomplish our goals in life. Negative beliefs get in the way of our success. Robbins reminds us that we can change our beliefs and choose new ones if necessary.

> *The birth of excellence begins with our awareness that our beliefs are a choice. We usually do not think of it that way, but belief can be a conscious choice. You can choose beliefs that limit you, or you can choose beliefs that support you. The trick is to choose the beliefs that are conducive to success and the results you want and to discard the ones that hold you back.*[10]

"If I believe I cannot do something, it makes me incapable of doing it. But when I believe I can, then I acquire the ability to do it, even if I did not have the ability in the beginning."

MAHATMA GANDHI

Beliefs cause us to have certain expectations about the world and ourselves. These expectations are such a powerful influence on behavior that psychologists use the term "self-fulfilling prophecy" to describe what happens when our expectations come true.

For example, if I believe that I am not good in math (my expectation), I may not try to do the assignment or may avoid taking a math class (my behavior). As a result, I am not good in math. My expectations have been fulfilled. Expectations can also have a positive effect. If I believe that I am a good student, I will take steps to enroll in college and complete my assignments. I will then become a good student. The prophecy will again come true.

Psychologist Robert Rosenthal has done some interesting research on the self-fulfilling prophecy.[11] Students in an elementary school were given an IQ test. Researchers told the teachers that this was a test that would determine "intellectual blooming." An experimental group of these students was chosen at random and teachers were told to expect remarkable gains in intellectual achievement in these children during the next eight months. At the end of this time, researchers gave the IQ test again. Students in the experimental group in which the teachers expected "intellectual blooming" actually gained higher IQ points than the control group. In addition, teachers described these students as more "interesting, curious and happy" than the control group. The teachers' expectations resulted in a self-fulfilling prophecy.

To think positively, it is necessary to recognize your negative beliefs and turn them into positive beliefs. Some negative beliefs commonly heard from college students include the following:

*I don't have the money for college.*
*English was never my best subject.*
*I was never any good at math.*

When you hear yourself saying these negative thoughts, remember that these thoughts can become self-fulfilling prophecies. First of all, notice the thought. Then see if you can change the statement into a positive statement such as:

*I can find the money for college.*
*English has been a challenge for me in the past, but I will do better this time.*
*I can learn to be good at math.*

If you believe that you can find money for college, you can go to the financial aid office and the scholarship office to begin your search for money to attend school. You can look for a better job or improve your money management. If you believe that you will do better in English, you will keep up with your assignments and ask the teacher for help. If you believe that you can learn to be good at math, you will attend every math class and seek tutoring when you do not understand. Your positive thoughts will help you to be successful.

> "Human beings can alter their lives by altering their attitude of mind."
> WILLIAM JAMES

## Visualize Your Success

Visualization is a powerful tool for taking control of your future as well as using your brain to improve memory, deal with stress, and think positively. Coaches and athletes study sports psychology to learn how to use visualization along with physical practice to improve athletic performance. College students can use the same techniques to enhance college success.

© SERGEY NIVENS/SHUTTERSTOCK.COM

> "The future first exists in imagination, then planning, then reality."
> R.A. WILSON

If you are familiar with sports or are an athlete, you can probably think of times when your coach asked you to use visualization to improve your performance. In baseball, the coach reminds players to keep their eye on the ball and visualize hitting it. In swimming, the coach asks swimmers to visualize reaching their arms out to touch the edge of the pool at the end of the race. Pole-vaulters visualize clearing the pole and sometimes even go through the motions before making the jump. Using imagery lets you practice for future events and pre-experience achieving your goals. Athletes imagine winning the race or completing the perfect jump in figure skating. In this way they prepare mentally and physically and develop confidence in their abilities.

Just as the athlete visualizes and then performs, the college student can do the same. It is said we create all things twice. First we make a mental picture and then we create the physical reality by taking action. For example, if we are building a house, we first get the idea, then we begin to design the house we want. We start with a blueprint and then build the house. The blueprint determines what kind of house we construct. The same thing happens in any project we undertake. First we have a mental picture and then we complete the project. Visualize what you would like to accomplish in your life as if you were creating a blueprint. Then take the steps to accomplish what you want.

As a college student, you might visualize yourself in your graduation robe walking across the stage to receive your diploma. You might visualize yourself in the exam room confidently taking the exam. You might see yourself on the job enjoying your future career. You can make a mental picture of what you would like your life to be and then work toward accomplishing your goal.

## Journal Entry

What tools can you use to take control of your life and create the future you want? How can you use locus of control, successful beliefs, hope, or visualization to accomplish your goals?

**4**

## Quiz

### Taking Control

1. Increase your chances of success by
   a. using external locus of control.
   b. using internal locus of control.
   c. believing that luck or fate controls your destiny.

2. The following is a statement showing internal locus of control:
   a. When bad things happen, there is not much you can do about it.
   b. Much of what happens is due to fate, chance, or luck.
   c. I can be successful through hard work.

**3.** Successful beliefs include the following:

    **a.** Put first things last.

    **b.** Begin with the end in mind.

    **c.** Think win-lose.

**4.** The _____ we have about ourselves determine much of our potential.

    **a.** beliefs

    **b.** doubts

    **c.** criticism

**5.** The statement, "We create all things twice," refers to

    **a.** doing the task twice to make sure it is done right.

    **b.** creating and refining.

    **c.** first making a mental picture and then taking action.

**How did you do on the quiz? Check your answers: 1. b, 2. c, 3. b, 4. a, 5. c**

# Secrets to Happiness

Many of you probably have happiness on your list of lifetime goals. It sounds easy, right? But what is happiness, anyway?

    Psychologist Martin Seligman says that real happiness comes from identifying, cultivating, and using your personal strengths in work, love, play, and parenting."[12] You can identify these strengths by learning about your personality type, interests, and values. Seligman contrasts authentic happiness with hedonism. He states that a hedonist "wants as many good moments and as few bad moments as possible in life."[13] Hedonism is a shortcut to happiness that leaves us feeling empty. For example, we often assume that more material possessions will make us happy. However, the more material possessions we have, the greater the expectations, and we no longer appreciate what we have.

    Most people assume that happiness is increased by having more money to buy that new car or HDTV. However, a process called hedonistic adaptation occurs, which makes this type of happiness short lived. Once you have purchased the new car or TV, you get used to it quickly. Soon you will start to think about a better car and a bigger TV to continue to feel happy. Seligman provides a formula for happiness[14]:

$$Happiness = S + C + V$$

In the formula $S$ stands for set range. Psychologists believe that 50 percent of happiness is determined by heredity. In other words, half of your level of happiness is determined by the genes inherited from your ancestors. In good times or bad times, people generally return to their set range of happiness. Six months after receiving a piece of good fortune such as a raise, promotion, or winning the lottery, unhappy people are still unhappy. Six months after a tragedy, naturally happy people return to being happy.

    The letter $C$ in the equation stands for circumstances such as money, marriage, social life, health, education, climate, race, gender, and religion.

"The three grand essentials of happiness are: something to do, someone to love, and something to hope for."
THOMAS CHALMERS

"Success is getting what you want; happiness is wanting what you get."
DALE CARNEGIE

These circumstances account for 8 to 15 percent of happiness. Here is what psychologists know about how these circumstances affect happiness:

- Once basic needs are met, greater wealth does not increase happiness.
- Having a good marriage is related to increased happiness.
- Happy people are more social.
- Moderate ill health does not bring unhappiness, but severe illness does.
- Educated people are slightly happier.
- Climate, race, and gender do not affect level of happiness.
- Religious people are somewhat happier than nonreligious people.

The letter $V$ in the equation stands for factors under your voluntary control. These factors account for approximately 40 percent of happiness. Factors under voluntary control include positive emotions and optimism about the future. Positive emotions include hope, faith, trust, joy, ecstasy, calm, zest, ebullience, pleasure, flow, satisfaction, contentment, fulfillment, pride, and serenity. Seligman suggests the following ideas to increase your positive emotions:

- Realize that the past does not determine your future. The future is open to new possibilities.
- Be grateful for the good events of the past and place less emphasis on the bad events.
- Build positive emotions through forgiving and forgetting.
- Work on increasing optimism and hope for the future.
- Find out what activities make you happy and engage in them. Spread these activities out over time so that you will not get tired of them.
- Take the time to savor the happy times. Make mental photographs of happy times so that you can think of them later.
- Take time to enjoy the present moment.
- Build more flow into your life. Flow is the state of gratification we feel when totally absorbed in an activity that matches our strengths.

Are you interested in taking steps to increase your happiness? Here are some activities proposed by Sonya Lyubomirsky, a leading researcher on happiness and author of *The How of Happiness*.[15] Choose the ones that seem like a natural fit for you and vary them so that they do not become routine or boring. After putting in some effort to practice these activities, they can become a habit.

1. **Express gratitude.** Expressing gratitude is a way of thinking positively and appreciating good circumstances rather than focusing on the bad ones. It is about appreciating and thanking the people who have made a positive contribution to your life. It is feeling grateful for the good things you have

in life. Create a gratitude journal and at the end of each day write down things for which you are grateful or thankful. Regularly tell those around you how grateful you are to have them in your life. You can do this in person, by phone, in a letter, or by email. Being grateful helps us to savor positive life experiences.

2.  **Cultivate optimism.** Make it a habit of looking at the bright side of life. If you think positively about the future, you are more likely to make the effort to reach your goals in life. Spend some time thinking or writing about your best possible future. Make a mental picture of your future goals as a first step toward achieving them. Thinking positively boosts your mood and promotes high morale. Most importantly, thinking positively can become a self-fulfilling prophecy. If you see your positive goals as attainable, you are more likely to work toward accomplishing them and invest the energy needed to deal with obstacles and setbacks along the way.

3.  **Avoid overthinking and social comparison.** Overthinking is focusing on yourself and your problems endlessly, needlessly, and excessively. Examples of overthinking include, "Why am I so unhappy?", "Why is life so unfair?", or "Why did he/she say that?". Overthinking increases sadness, fosters biased thinking, decreases motivation, and makes it difficult to solve problems and take action to make life better.

    Social comparison is a type of overthinking. In our daily lives, we encounter people who are more intelligent, beautiful, richer, healthier, or happier. The media fosters images of people with impossibly perfect lives. Making social comparisons can lead to feelings of inferiority and loss of self-esteem.

    Notice when your are overthinking or making comparisons with others and stop doing it. Use the yell "Stop" technique to refocus your attention. This technique involves yelling "Stop" to yourself or out loud to change your thinking. Another way to stop overthinking is to distract yourself with more positive thoughts or activities. Watch a funny movie, listen to music, or arrange a social activity with a friend. If these activities are not effective, try writing down your worries in a journal. Writing helps to organize thoughts and to make sense of them. Begin to take some small steps to resolve your worries and problems.

4. **Practice acts of kindness.** Doing something kind for others increases your own personal happiness and satisfies our basic need for human connection. Opportunities for helping others surround us each day. How about being courteous on the freeway, helping a child with homework, or helping your elderly neighbor with yard work? A simple act of kindness makes you feel good and often sets off a chain of events in which the person who receives the kindness does something kind for someone else.

5. **Increase flow activities.** Flow is defined as intense involvement in an activity so that you do not notice the passage of time. Musicians are in the flow when they are totally involved in their music. Athletes are in the flow when they are totally focused on their sport. Writers are in the flow when they are totally absorbed in writing down their ideas. The key to achieving flow is balancing skills and challenges. If your skills are not sufficient for the activity, you will become frustrated. If your skills are greater than what is demanded for the activity, you will become bored. Work often provides an opportunity to experience flow if you are in a situation in which your work activities are matched to your skills and talents.

As our skills increase, it becomes more difficult to maintain flow. We must be continually testing ourselves in ever more challenging activities to maintain flow. You can take some action to increase the flow in your life by learning to fully focus your attention on the activity you are doing. It is important to be open to new and different experiences. To maintain the flow in your life, make a commitment to lifelong learning.

6. **Savor life's joys.** Savoring is the repetitive replaying of the positive experiences in life and is one of the most important ingredients of happiness. Savoring happens in the past, present, and future. Think often about the good things that have happened in the past. Savor the present by relishing the present moment. Savor the future by anticipating and visualizing positive events or outcomes in the future.

There are many ways to savor life's joys. Replay in your mind happy days or events from the past. Create a photo album of your favorite people, places, and events and look at it often. This prolongs the happiness. Take a few minutes each day to appreciate ordinary activities such as taking a shower or walking to work. Engage the senses to notice your environment. Is it a sunny day? Take some time to look at the sky, the trees, and plants. Landscape architects incorporate art work, trees, and flowers along the

> "Finish each day and be done with it. You have done what you could; some blunders and absurdities have crept in; forget them as soon as you can. Tomorrow is a new day; you shall begin it serenely and with too high a spirit to be encumbered with your old nonsense."
> RALPH WALDO EMERSON

freeways to help drivers to relax on the road. Notice art and objects of beauty. Be attentive to the present moment and be aware of your surroundings. Picture in your mind positive events you anticipate in the future. All of these activities will increase your "psychological bank account" of happy times and will help you deal with times that are not so happy.

7. **Commit to accomplishing your goals.** Working toward a meaningful life goal is one of the most important things that you can do to have a happy life. Goals provide structure and meaning to our lives and improve self-esteem. Working on goals provides something to look forward to in the future.

   The types of goals that you pursue have an impact on your happiness. The goals that have the most potential for long-term happiness involve changing your activities rather than changing your circumstances. Examples of goals that change your circumstances are moving to the beach or buying a new stereo. These goals make you happy for a short time. Then you get used to your new circumstances and no longer feel as happy as when you made the initial change. Examples of goals that change your activities are returning to school or taking up a new sport or hobby. These activities allow you to take on new challenges that keep life interesting for a longer period of time. Choose intrinsic goals that help you to develop your competence and autonomy. These goals should match your most important values and interests.

> "Happiness consists more in small conveniences or pleasures that occur every day, than in great pieces of good fortune that happen but seldom."
> BENJAMIN FRANKLIN

8. **Take care of your body.** Engaging in physical activity provides many opportunities for increasing happiness. Physical activity helps to:
   • Increase longevity and improve the quality of life.
   • Improve sleep and protect the body from disease.
   • Keep brains healthy and avoid cognitive impairments.
   • Increase self-esteem.
   • Increase the opportunity to engage in flow.
   • Provide a distraction from worries and overthinking.

> "An aim in life is the only fortune worth finding."
> ROBERT LOUIS STEVENSON

© GPOINTSTUDIO/SHUTTERSTOCK.COM

David Myers, a professor of psychology at Hope College in Michigan, is a leading researcher on happiness. He says that 90 percent of us are naturally happy. He adds that if most of us "were characteristically unhappy, the emotional pain would lose its ability to alert us to an unusual and possibly harmful condition."[16]

Just as you have made a decision to get a college degree, make a decision to be happy. Make a decision to be happy by altering your internal outlook and choosing to change your behavior. Here are some suggestions for consciously choosing happiness.

1. Find small things that make you happy and sprinkle your life with them. A glorious sunset, a pat on the back, a well-manicured yard, an unexpected gift, a round of tennis, a favorite sandwich, a fishing line cast on a quiet lake, the wagging tail of the family dog, or your child finally taking some responsibility—these are things that will help to create a continual climate of happiness.

2. Smile and stand up straight. Michael Mercer and Maryann Troiani, authors of *Spontaneous Optimism: Proven Strategies for Health, Prosperity and Happiness*, say that "unhappy people tend to slouch, happy people don't. . . . Happy people even take bigger steps when they walk."[17]

3. Learn to think like an optimist. "Pessimists tend to complain; optimists focus on solving their problems."[18] Never use the word "try"; this word is for pessimists. Assume you will succeed.

4. Replace negative thoughts with positive ones.

5. Fill your life with things you like to do.

6. Get enough rest. If you do not get enough sleep, you will feel tired and gloomy. Sleep deprivation can lead to depression.

7. Learn from your elders. Psychologist Daniel Mroczek says that "people in their sixties and seventies who are in good health are among the happiest people in our society. . . . They may be better able to regulate their emotions, they've developed perspective, they don't get so worried about little things, and they've often achieved their goals and aren't trying to prove themselves."[19]

8. Reduce stress.

9. Take charge of your time by doing first things first.

10. Close relationships are important. Myers and Mroczek report higher levels of happiness among married men and women.[20]

11. Keep things in perspective. Will it matter in six months to a year?

12. Laugh more. Laughter produces a relaxation response.

## Journal
### Entry

What does happiness mean to you? Write five intention statements regarding your future happiness.

To me happiness is . . .

I intend to . . .

**5**

© ANSON0618/SHUTTERSTOCK.COM

## Keys to Success

### Learn to Laugh at Life

*"Have a laugh at life and look around you for happiness instead of sadness. Laughter has always brought me out of unhappy situations. Even in your darkest moment, you usually can find something to laugh about if you try hard enough."*
RED SKELTON

All of us face challenges in life, but if we can learn the gift of laughter and have a good sense of humor, it is easier to deal with these challenges and create the future we want to have. Laughter has important physical as well as emotional benefits. Laughter relaxes the body, boosts the immune system, and even improves the function of blood vessels and

© DIRK ERCKEN/SHUTTERSTOCK.COM

increases blood flow, which can protect the heart. It adds joy and zest to life, reduces anxiety, relieves stress, improves mood, and enhances resilience. Being more relaxed can even help you to shift perspective, solve problems, and be more creative.

Just putting a smile on your face can help. German psychologist Fritz Strack had his subjects watch a cartoon with a pencil in their mouths. Half of his subjects held the pencil between their teeth, which made them laugh. The other half of his subjects held the pencil between their lips, which made them frown. The smiling group thought that the cartoon was funnier. It seems that there is a connection between our physical responses and our internal feelings. The physical act of smiling actually makes you feel happier.[21]

If you do not feel happy, smile and pretend to feel happy. Neurophysicist Richard Hamilton says that if you pretend to be happy, you actually feel better, because positive thoughts and behavior impact the biochemistry of the brain. Positive thinking helps the brain produce seratonin, a neurotransmitter linked with feelings of happiness.[22]

Humor has several components. Humor involves looking at the incongruities of life and laughing at them. It is looking at adversity and finding the humor in the situation. It is a playful attitude and the ability to make other people smile. Most children are play-ful, but socialization reduces their playfulness. You can develop your sense of humor by taking your-self less seriously and being grateful for the good things in your life. Learn to laugh at yourself by sharing your embarassing moments and laughing at them. Be careful not to use humor that puts down other people or groups. Surround yourself with people who enjoy humor and laughter. Look for the humor in difficult situations. Life is full of irony and absurdity and laughing about it unites people during difficult times. By laughing at the situation, you will be in a better position to deal with it. Keep a positive perspective by focusing on the good things that are happening in your life rather than dwelling on the negatives.

The author, Mark Twain, was a good example of using humor in life. Mark Twain said that he had never worked a day in his life. He said, "What I have done I have done because it has been play. If it had been work, I shouldn't have done it." He used humor throughout his life despite facing many adversities. His father died when he was 11 years old and he started work at age 12 as a printer's apprentice. He was constantly in trouble and spent some time in jail. He served in the Civil War. His wife died at an early age and three out of four of his children died before he did.

As a child, he enjoyed playing pranks on his mother and she responded with a sense of humor. After playing a prank on his mother, she told him that he gave her more trouble than all the other children. He replied, "I suppose you were afraid I wouldn't live," and she responded, "No: afraid you would." When Mark Train almost drowned in the river, she pulled him out and said, "I guess there wasn't much danger. People born to be hanged are safe in water." Mark Twain's children described him as "a very good man and a very funny one. . . . He does tell perfectly delightful stories." He started every day by making jokes at the breakfast table and his humor is later reflected in his famous books, including *Huckleberry Finn* and *Tom Sawyer*. He wrote that "humor is a great thing . . . the saving thing after all. The minute it crops up, all our hardnesses yield, all our irritations, and resentments flit away, and a sunny spirit takes their place."[23]

The path to achieving your goals is much smoother if you choose to be happy. So relax, smile, and be happy. Then work on making positive changes in your life.

## JOURNAL ENTRIES
## CREATE YOUR SUCCESS

Go to http://www.collegesuccess1.com/JournalEntries.htm for Word files of the Journal Entries.

# SUCCESS
## over the Internet

**Visit the *College Success Website* at http://www.collegesuccess1. com/**

The *College Success Website* is continually updated with new topics and links to the material presented in this chapter. Topics include:

- Choosing a major
- Motivation
- Education and earnings
- Positive thinking
- Emotional intelligence
- Happiness

Contact your instructor if you have any problems in accessing the *College Success Website*.

# Notes

1. Federal Reserve Bank of New York, "Do the Benefits of College Still Outweigh the Costs?" *Current Issues in Economics and Finance* 20, no. 3 (2014): 1–9. http://www.newyorkfed.org/research/current-issues.
2. US Bureau of Labor Statistics, "Unemployment Rates and Earnings by Educational Attainment," last modified September 1, 2020, https://www.bls.gov/emp/tables/unemployment-earnings-education.htm.
3. Christopher Peterson, *A Primer in Positive Psychology* (New York: Oxford University Press, 2006), 127.
4. Daniel Goleman, "Hope Emerges a Key to Success in Life," *New York Times*, December 1991, 24.
5. M. J. Findlay and H. M. Cooper, "Locus of Control and Academic Achievement: A Literature Review," *Journal of Personality and Social Psychology 44* (1983): 419–427.
6. Stephen R. Covey, *The 7 Habits of Highly Effective People* (New York: Simon and Schuster, 1989).
7. Stephen R. Covey, *The 8th Habit, from Effectiveness to Greatness* (New York: Free Press, 2004).
8. Ibid.
9. Anthony Robbins, *Unlimited Power* (New York: Fawcett Columbine, 1986), 54–55.
10. Ibid., 57.
11. Robert Rosenthal, "Self-Fulfilling Prophecy," *Psychology Today,* September 1968.
12. Martin Seligman, *Authentic Happiness, Using the New Positive Psychology to Realize Your Potential for Lasting Fulfillment.* (New York: Free Press, 2002), xiii.
13. Ibid., 6.
14. Ibid., 45.

15. Sonya Lyubomirsky, *The How of Happiness* (New York: The Penguin Press, 2008).

16. Quoted in Joan Smith, "Nineteen Habits of Happy Women," *Redbook Magazine,* August 1999, 66.

17. Quoted in Smith, "Nineteen Habits of Happy Women."

18. Ibid.

19. Ibid.

20. Ibid.

21. Ibid., 68.

22. Ibid.

23. Christopher Peterson and Martin Seligman, *Character Strengths and Virtues; A Handbook and Classification* (Oxford: University Press, 2004), 583–584.

# BEGIN WITH SELF-ASSESSMENT

A good way to begin this course is to assess your present skills to determine your strengths and areas that need improvement. Complete the following assessment to get an overview of the topics presented in the textbook and to measure your present skills.

## Measure Your Success

The following statements represent major topics included in the textbook. Read the following statements and rate how true they are for you at the present time. At the end of the course, you will have the opportunity to complete this assessment again to measure your progress.

5   Definitely true
4   Mostly true
3   Somewhat true
2   Seldom true
1   Never true

_____ I understand the steps in choosing a major and career.

_____ I understand how education will affect my future earnings.

_____ I know how to use motivation techniques to be successful.

_____ I have control over my life and can create my future.

_____ I usually practice positive thinking.

_____ I have a visual picture of my future success.

_____ I have a clear idea of what happiness means to me.

_____ Total points for Creating Success

_____ I can describe my personality type.

_____ I can list careers that match my personality type.

_____ I can describe my personal strengths and talents based on my personality type.

_____ I understand how my personality type affects how I manage my time and money.

_____ II know what college majors are most in demand.

_____ I am confident that I have chosen the best major for myself.

_____ Courses related to my major are interesting and exciting to me.

_____ Total points for Personality and Major

_____ I can describe my vocational interests.

_____ I can list careers that match my vocational interests.

_____ I can list my top five values.

_____ I generally consider my most important values when making decisions.

_____ My actions are generally guided by my personal values.

_____ My personal values motivate me to be successful.

_____ I can balance work, study, and leisure activities.

_____ Total points for Interests and Values

_____ I understand how my mindset affects my intelligences.

_____ I understand how grit and perseverance affect my intelligences.

_____ I understand the concept of multiple intelligences.

_____ I can list my multiple intelligences.

_____ I can list the careers that match my intelligences.

_____ I am aware of my emotional intelligence and use it to create positive relationships.

_____ I believe that I can create my own future.

_____ Total points for Multiple Intelligences

_____ I understand how current employment trends will affect my future.

_____ I can list my highest job skills and those that need improvement.

_____ I know how to do career research.

_____ I am aware of the job outlook for careers in which I am interested.

_____ I have an educational plan that matches my academic and career goals.

_____ I know the steps in making a good career decision.

_____ I know how to match my career to my personality, interests, values, intelligences, and skills.

_____ Total points for Career and Education

_____ I know how to increase my chances for employment while in college.

_____ I know how to write a good resume and cover letter.

_____ I understand personal branding and know how to market myself online.

_____ I know how to use social media to find a job.

_____ I am familiar with online tools for job search.

_____ I know how to interview for a job.

_____ I know about options for creating my own business.

_____ Total points for Job Search Strategies

_____ I know how to find passion and meaning in my work.

_____ I understand the role of money in my own career satisfaction.

_____ I know about the predictors of job satisfaction.

_____ I can identify what makes people happy at work.

_____ I know how to be successful on the job.

_____ I have some specific and achievable goals for the future.

_____ I use priorities in managing my time to accomplish my future goals.

_____ Total Points for Career Satisfaction

Total your points

_____ Creating Success

_____ Personality and Major

_____ Interests and Values

_____ Multiple Intelligences and Goal Setting

_____ Career and Education

_____ Job Search Strategies

_____ Career Satisfaction

_____ Grand total points

If you scored

| | |
|---|---|
| 221-245 | You have excellent skills for creating your future career, but you can always learn something new. |
| 220-197 | You have good skills for creating your future career, but could improve. |
| 196-173 | You have average skills for creating your future career, but will increase your skills in this course. |
| Below 172 | Your score is low right now, but this course will help you to increase the skills for creating your future career. |

What are the areas in which your scored the highest?




What areas do you need to improve?

# SUCCESS WHEEL

Use your scores from "Measure Your Success to complete the following success wheel. You different colored markers to shade in each section of the wheel.

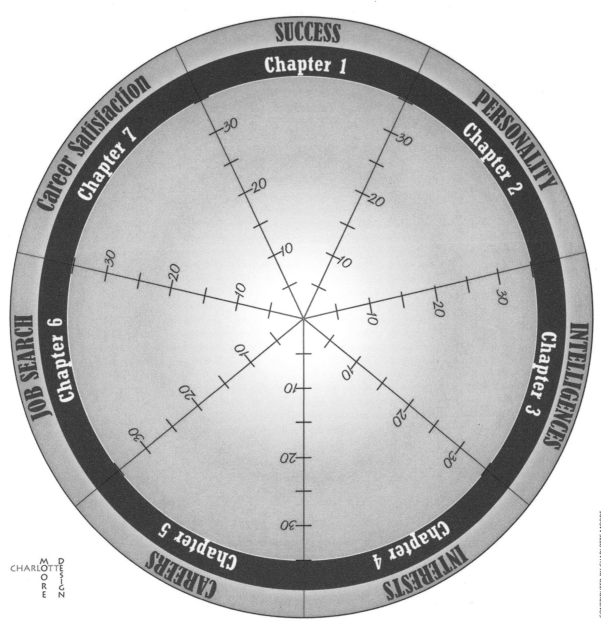

CONTRIBUTED BY CHARLOTTE MOORE.
COPYRIGHT © KENDALL HUNT PUBLISHING COMPANY.

# Visualize Your Success

To be successful, you will need a clear mental picture of what success means to you. Take a few minutes to create a mental picture of what success means to you. Include your education, career, family life, lifestyle, finances, and anything else that is important to you. Make your picture as a specific and detailed as possible. Write about this picture or draw it in the space below. You may wish to use a mind map, list, outline, or sentences to describe your picture of success.

# Happiness Is...

Think of small things and big things that make you happy. List or draw them in the space below.

# Exploring Your Personality and Major 2

## Learning
## OBJECTIVES

Read to answer these key questions:

- What are the different personality types?

- What is my personality type?

- What are my personal strengths?

- How is personality type related to choice of a major and career?

- What are the characteristics of my ideal career?

- What careers and majors should I consider based on my personality type?

- What are some other factors in choosing a major?

To assure your success in college, it is important to choose the major that is best for you. If you choose a major and career that match your personality, interests, aptitudes, and values, you will enjoy your studies and excel in your work. It was Picasso who said that you know you enjoy your work when you do not notice the time passing by. If you can become interested in your work and studies, you are on your way to developing passion and joy in your life. If you can get up each morning and enjoy the work that you do (at least on most days), you will surely have one of the keys to happiness.

## Choose a Major That Matches Your Gifts and Talents

The first step in choosing the major that is right for you is to understand your personality type. Psychologists have developed useful theories of personality that can help you understand how personality type relates to the choice of major and career. The personality theory used in this textbook is derived from the work of Swiss psychologist Carl Jung (1875–1961). Jung believed that we are born with a predisposition for certain personality preferences and that healthy development is based on the lifelong nurturing of inborn preferences rather than trying to change a person to become something different. Each personality type has gifts and talents that can be nurtured over a lifetime.

"To be what we are, and to become what we are capable of becoming, is the only end of life."
ROBERT LOUIS STEVENSON

The theories of Carl Jung were further developed by American psychologists Katherine Briggs and her daughter Isabel Myers, who created the Myers-Briggs Type Indicator (MBTI) to measure different personality types. The connection between personality type and career choice was established through statistical analysis. The TruTalent Personality online assessment is based on the practical application of the theories of these psychologists.

While assessments are not exact predictors of your future major and career, they provide useful information that will get you started on the path of career exploration and finding the college major that is best suited to you. Knowledge of your personality and the personalities of others is not only valuable in understanding yourself, but also in appreciating how others are different. This understanding of self and others will empower you to communicate and work effectively with others. Complete the TruTalent Personality assessment that is included with this textbook before you begin this chapter. (See the inside front cover for information on accessing this assessment.)

## Understanding Personality Types

Just as no two fingerprints or snowflakes are exactly alike, each person is a different and unique individual. Even with this uniqueness, however, we can make some general statements about personality. When we make generalizations, we are talking about averages. These averages can provide useful information about ourselves and other people, but it is important to remember that no individual is exactly described by the average. As you read through the following descriptions of personality types, keep in mind that we are talking about generalizations or beginning points for discussion and thoughtful analysis.

As you read through your personality description from the TruTalent Personality assessment and the information in this text, **focus on your personal strengths and talents.** Building on these personal strengths has several important benefits. It increases self-esteem and self-confidence, which contribute to your success and enjoyment of life. Building on your strengths provides the energy and motivation required to put in the effort needed to accomplish any worthwhile task. The assessment also identifies some of your possible weaknesses or "blind spots." Just be aware of these blind spots so that they do not interfere with your success. Being aware of your blind spots can even be used to your advantage. For example, some personality types thrive by working with people. A career that involves much public contact is a good match for this personality type, whereas choosing a career where public contact is limited can lead to job dissatisfaction. Knowing about your personality type can help you make the right decisions to maximize your potential.

Based on the work of Carl Jung, Katherine Briggs, and Isabel Myers, personality has four dimensions:

1. Extraversion or Introversion
2. Sensing or Intuition
3. Thinking or Feeling
4. Judging or Perceiving

These dimensions of personality will be defined and examined in more depth in the sections that follow.

## Extraversion or Introversion

The dimension of extraversion or introversion defines how we interact with the world and how our energy flows. In the general school population, 75 percent of students are usually extraverts and 25 percent are introverts.

*Extraverts (E)* focus their energy on the world outside themselves. They enjoy interaction with others and get to know a lot of different people. They enjoy and are usually good at communication. They are energized by social interaction and prefer being active. These types are often described as talkative and social.

*Introverts (I)* focus their energy on the world inside of themselves. They enjoy spending time alone to think about the world in order to understand it. Introverts prefer more limited social contacts, choosing smaller groups or one-on-one relationships. These types are often described as quiet or reserved.

We all use the introvert and extravert modes while functioning in our daily lives. Whether a person is an extravert or an introvert is a matter of preference, like being left- or right-handed. We can use our nondominant hand, but it is not as comfortable as using our dominant hand. We are usually more skillful in using the dominant hand. For example, introverts can learn to function well in social situations, but later may need some peace and quiet to recharge. On the other hand, social contact energizes the extravert.

**One personality type is not better than the other: it is just different.** Being an extravert is not better than being an introvert. Each type has unique gifts and talents that can be used in different occupations. An extravert might enjoy working in an occupation with lots of public contact, such as being a receptionist or handling public relations. An introvert might enjoy being an accountant or writer. However, as with all of the personality dimensions, a person may have traits of both types.

# Activity

## Introverts and Extraverts

The list below describes some qualities of introverts and extraverts. **For each pair of items,** quickly choose the phrase that describes you best and place a checkmark next to it. Remember that one type is not better than another. You may also find that you are a combination type and act like an introvert in some situations and an extravert in others. Each type has gifts and talents that can be used in choosing the best major and career for you. To get an estimate of your preference, notice which column has the most checkmarks.

| **Introvert (I)** | **Extravert (E)** |
|---|---|
| _____ Energized by having quiet time alone | _____ Energized by social interaction |
| _____ Tend to think first and talk later | _____ Tend to talk first and think later |
| _____ Tend to think things through quietly | _____ Tend to think out loud |
| _____ Tend to respond slowly, after thinking | _____ Tend to respond quickly, before thinking |
| _____ Avoid being the center of attention | _____ Like to be the center of attention |
| _____ Difficult to get to know, private | _____ Easy to get to know, outgoing |
| _____ Have a few close friends | _____ Have many friends, know lots of people |
| _____ Prefer quiet for concentration | _____ Can read or talk with background noise |
| _____ Listen more than talk | _____ Talk more than listen |
| _____ View telephone calls as a distraction | _____ View telephone calls as a welcome break |
| _____ Talk to a few people at parties | _____ Talk to many different people at parties |
| _____ Share special occasions with one or a few people | _____ Share special occasions with large groups |
| _____ Prefer to study alone | _____ Prefer to study with others in a group |
| _____ Prefer the library to be quiet | _____ Talk with others in the library |
| _____ Described as quiet or reserved | _____ Described as talkative or friendly |
| _____ Work systematically | _____ Work through trial and error |

Here are some qualities that describe the ideal work environment. Again, as you read through each pair of items, place a checkmark next to the work environment that you prefer.

**Introvert (I)**

_____ Work alone or with individuals

_____ Quiet for concentration

_____ Communication one-on-one

_____ Work in small groups

_____ Focus on one project until complete

_____ Work without interruption

_____ **Total** (from both charts above)

**Extravert (E)**

_____ Much public contact

_____ High-energy environment

_____ Present ideas to a group

_____ Work as part of a team

_____ Variety and action

_____ Talk to others

_____ **Total** (from both charts above)

Do these results agree with your TruTalent Personality assessment? If your results are the same, this is a good indication that your results are useful and accurate. Are there some differences with the results obtained from your personality assessment? If your results are different, this provides an opportunity for further reflection about your personality type. Here are a couple of reasons why your results may be different.

1. You may be a combination type with varying degrees of preference for each type.

2. You may have chosen your personality type on the TruTalent Personality assessment based on what you think is best rather than what you truly are. Students sometimes do this because of the myth that there are good and bad personality types. It is important to remember that each personality type has strengths and weaknesses. By identifying strengths, you can build on them by choosing the right major and career. By being aware of weaknesses, you can come up with strategies to compensate for them to be successful.

Look at the total number of checkmarks for extravert and introvert on the two above charts. Do you lean toward being an introvert or an extravert? Remember that one type is not better than the other and each has unique gifts and talents. On the chart below, place an X on the line to indicate how much you prefer introversion or extraversion. If you selected most of the introvert traits, place your X somewhere on the left side. If you selected most of the extravert traits, place your X somewhere on the right side. If you are equally introverted and extraverted, place your X in the middle.

Introvert _____|_____ Extravert

Do you generally prefer introversion or extraversion? In the box below, write **I** for introversion or **E** for extraversion. If there is a tie between **E** and **I**, write **I**.

Notice that it is possible to be a combination type. At times you might prefer to act like an introvert, and at other times you might prefer to act like an extravert. It is beneficial to be able to balance these traits. However, for combination types, it is more difficult to select specific occupations that match this type

## Journal Entry

Look at the results from the TruTalent Personality assessment and your own self-assessment above. Are you an introvert or an extravert or a combination of these two types? Can you give examples of how it affects your social life, school, or work? Write a paragraph about this preference.

## Sensing or Intuition

The dimension of sensing or intuition describes how we take in information. In the general school population, 70 percent of students are usually sensing types and 30 percent are intuitive types.

*Sensing (S) persons prefer to use the senses to take in information (what they see, hear, taste, touch, smell). They focus on "what is" and trust information that is concrete and observable. They learn through experience.*

*Intuitive (N) persons rely on instincts and focus on "what could be." While we all use our five senses to perceive the world, intuitive people are interested in relationships, possibilities, meanings, and implications. They value inspiration and trust their "sixth sense" or hunches. (Intuitive is designated as N so it is not confused with I for Introvert.)*

We all use both of these modes in our daily lives, but we usually have a preference for one mode or the other. Again, there is no best preference. Each type has special skills that can be applied to the job market. For example, you would probably want your tax preparer to be a sensing type who focuses on concrete information and fills out your tax form correctly. An inventor or artist would probably be an intuitive type.

## Activity

### Sensing and Intuitive

Here are some qualities of sensing and intuitive persons. **As you read through each pair of items,** quickly place a checkmark next to the item that usually describes yourself.

| Sensing (S) | INtuitive (N) |
|---|---|
| _____ Trust what is certain and concrete | _____ Trust inspiration and inference |
| _____ Prefer specific answers to questions | _____ Prefer general answers that leave room for interpretation |
| _____ Like new ideas if they have practical applications (if you can use them) | _____ Like new ideas for their own sake (you don't need a practical use for them) |
| _____ Value realism and common sense | _____ Value imagination and innovation |

| | |
|---|---|
| _____ Think about things one at a time and step by step | _____ Think about many ideas at once as they come to you |
| _____ Like to improve and use skills learned before | _____ Like to learn new skills and get bored using the same skills |
| _____ More focused on the present | _____ More focused on the future |
| _____ Concentrate on what you are doing | _____ Wonder what is next |
| _____ Do something | _____ Think about doing something |
| _____ See tangible results | _____ Focus on possibilities |
| _____ If it isn't broken, don't fix it | _____ There is always a better way to do it |

**Sensing (S)** / **INtuitive (N)**

| | |
|---|---|
| _____ Prefer working with facts and figures | _____ Prefer working with ideas and theories |
| _____ Focus on reality | _____ Use fantasy |
| _____ Seeing is believing | _____ Anything is possible |
| _____ Tend to be specific and literal (say what you mean) | _____ Tend to be general and figurative (use comparisons and analogies) |
| _____ See what is here and now | _____ See the big picture |

Here are some qualities that describe the ideal work environment. Again, as you read through each pair of items,
place a checkmark next to the work environment that you prefer.

**Sensing (S)** / **INtuitive (N)**

| | |
|---|---|
| _____ Use and practice skills | _____ Learn new skills |
| _____ Work with known facts | _____ Explore new ideas and approaches |
| _____ See measurable results | _____ Work with theories |
| _____ Focus on practical benefits | _____ Use imagination and be original |
| _____ Learn through experience | _____ Freedom to follow your inspiration |
| _____ Pleasant environment | _____ Challenging environment |
| _____ Use standard procedures | _____ Invent new products and procedures |
| _____ Work step-by-step | _____ Work in bursts of energy |
| _____ Do accurate work | _____ Find creative solutions |
| _____ **Total** (from both charts above) | _____ **Total** (from both charts above) |

Look at the two charts above and see whether you tend to be more sensing or intuitive. One preference is not better than another: it is just different. On the chart below, place an X on the line to indicate your preference for sensing or intuitive. Again, notice that it is possible to be a combination type with both sensing and intuitive preferences.

Sensing _____|_____ Intuitive

Do you generally prefer sensing or intuition? In the box below, write **S** for sensing or **N** for intuitive. If there is a tie between **S** and **N**, write **N**.

## Journal Entry

Look at the results from the TruTalent Personality assessment and your own self-assessment above. Are you an introvert or an extravert or a combination of these two types? Can you give examples of how it affects your social life, school, or work? Write a paragraph about this preference.

**2**

## Thinking or Feeling

The dimension of thinking or feeling defines how we prefer to make decisions. In the general school population, 60 percent of males are thinking types and 40 percent are feeling types. For females, 60 percent are feeling types and 40 percent are thinking types.

*Thinking (T) individuals make decisions based on logic. They are objective and analytical. They look at all the evidence and reach an impersonal conclusion. They are concerned with* what they think is right.

*Feeling (F) individuals make decisions based on what is important to them and matches their personal values. They are concerned about* what they feel is right.

We all use logic and have feelings and emotions that play a part in decision making. However, the thinking person prefers to make decisions based on logic, and the feeling person prefers to make decisions according to what is important to self and others. This is one category in which men and women often differ. Most women are feeling types, and most men are logical types. When men and women are arguing, you might hear the following:

*Man: "I think that . . ."*

*Woman: "I feel that . . ."*

By understanding these differences, it is possible to improve communication and understanding. Be careful with generalizations, since 40 percent of men and women would not fit this pattern.

When thinking about careers, a thinking type would make a good judge or computer programmer. A feeling type would probably make a good social worker or kindergarten teacher.

# Activity

## Thinking and Feeling

The following chart shows some qualities of thinking and feeling types. **As you read through each pair of items**, quickly place a checkmark next to the items that usually describe yourself.

| Thinking (T) | Feeling (F) |
|---|---|
| _____ Apply impersonal analysis to problems | _____ Consider the effect on others |
| _____ Value logic and justice | _____ Value empathy and harmony |
| _____ Fairness is important | _____ There are exceptions to every rule |
| _____ Truth is more important than tact | _____ Tact is more important than truth |
| _____ Motivated by achievement and accomplishment | _____ Motivated by being appreciated by others |
| _____ Feelings are valid if they are logical or not | _____ Feelings are valid whether they make sense |
| _____ Good decisions are logical | _____ Good decisions take others' feelings into account |

| Thinking (T) | Feeling (F) |
|---|---|
| _____ Described as cool, calm, and objective | _____ Described as caring and emotional |
| _____ Love can be analyzed | _____ Love cannot be analyzed |
| _____ Firm-minded | _____ Gentle-hearted |
| _____ More important to be right | _____ More important to be liked |
| _____ Remember numbers and figures | _____ Remember faces and names |
| _____ Prefer clarity | _____ Prefer harmony |
| _____ Find flaws and critique | _____ Look for the good and compliment |
| _____ Prefer firmness | _____ Prefer persuasion |

Here are some qualities that describe the ideal work environment. As you read through each pair of items, place a checkmark next to the items that usually describe the work environment that you prefer.

| Thinking (T) | Feeling (F) |
|---|---|
| _____ Maintain business environment | _____ Maintain close personal relationships |
| _____ Work with people I respect | _____ Work in a friendly, relaxed environment |
| _____ Be treated fairly | _____ Be able to express personal values |
| _____ Fair evaluations | _____ Appreciation for good work |
| _____ Solve problems | _____ Make a personal contribution |
| _____ Challenging work | _____ Harmonious work situation |
| _____ Use logic and analysis | _____ Help others |
| _____ **Total** (from both charts above) | _____ **Total** (from both charts above) |

While we all use thinking and feeling, what is your preferred type? Look at the charts above and notice whether you are more the thinking or feeling type. One is not better than the other. On the chart below, place an X on the line to indicate how much you prefer thinking or feeling.

Thinking_____|_____ Feeling

Do you generally prefer thinking or feeling? In the box below, write **T** for thinking or **F** for feeling. If there is a tie between **T** and **F**, write **F**.

**Journal Entry**

Look at the results from the TruTalent Personality assessment and your own self-assessment above. Are you a thinking, feeling, or combination type? Can you give examples of how it affects your social life, school, or work? Write a paragraph about this preference.

**3**

## Judging or Perceiving

The dimension of judging or perceiving refers to how we deal with the external world. In other words, do we prefer the world to be structured or unstructured? In the general school population, the percentage of each of these types is approximately equal.

> *Judging (J) types like to live in a structured, orderly, and planned way. They are happy when their lives are structured and matters are settled. They like to have control over their lives. **Judging does not mean to judge others.** Think of this type as being orderly and organized.*

> *Perceptive (P) types like to live in a spontaneous and flexible way. They are happy when their lives are open to possibilities. They try to understand life rather than control it. **Think of this type as spontaneous and flexible.***

Since these types have very opposite ways of looking at the world, there is a great deal of potential for conflict between them unless there is an appreciation for the gifts and talents of both. In any situation, we can benefit from people who represent these very different points of view. For example, in a business situation, the judging type would be good at managing the money, while the perceptive type would be good at helping the business to adapt to a changing marketplace. It is good to be open to all the possibilities and to be flexible, as well as to have some structure and organization.

# Activity

## Judging and Perceptive

**As you read through each pair of items,** quickly place a checkmark next to the items that generally describe yourself.

**Judging (J)**

_____ Happy when the decisions are made and finished

_____ Work first, play later

_____ It is important to be on time

_____ Time flies

_____ Feel comfortable with routine

_____ Generally keep things in order

_____ Set goals and work toward them

_____ Emphasize completing the task

_____ Like to finish projects

_____ Meet deadlines

_____ Like to know what I am getting into

_____ Relax when things are organized

_____ Follow a routine

_____ Focused

_____ Work steadily

**Perceptive (P)**

_____ Happy when the options are left open; something better may come along

_____ Play first, do the work later

_____ Time is relative

_____ Time is elastic

_____ Dislike routine

_____ Prefer creative disorder

_____ Change goals as new opportunities arise

_____ Emphasize how the task is done

_____ Like to start projects

_____ What deadline?

_____ Like new possibilities and situations

_____ Relax when necessary

_____ Explore the unknown

_____ Easily distracted

_____ Work in spurts of energy

Here are some qualities that describe the ideal work environment. Again, as you **read through each pair of items,** place a checkmark next to the work environment that you prefer.

**Judging (J)**

_____ Follow a schedule

_____ Clear directions

_____ Organized work

_____ Logical order

_____ Control my job

_____ Stability and security

_____ Work on one project until done

_____ Steady work

_____ Satisfying work

**Perceptive (P)**

_____ Be spontaneous

_____ Minimal rules and structure

_____ Flexibility

_____ Many changes

_____ Respond to emergencies

_____ Take risks and be adventurous

_____ Juggle many projects

_____ Variety and action

_____ Fun and excitement

_____  Like having high responsibility       _____  Like having interesting work

_____  Accomplish goals on time              _____  Work at my own pace

_____  Clear and concrete assignments        _____  Minimal supervision

_____  **Total** (from both charts above)     _____  **Total** (from both charts above)

Look at the charts above and notice whether you are more the judging type (orderly and organized) or the perceptive type (spontaneous and flexible). We need the qualities of both types to be successful and deal with the rapid changes in today's world. On the chart below, place an X on the line to indicate how much you prefer judging or perceiving.

Judging _____|_____ Perceptive

Do you generally have judging or perceptive traits? In the box below, write **J** for judging or **P** for perceptive. If there is a tie between **J** and **P**, write **P**.

[ ]

## Journal
## Entry

Look at the results from the TruTalent Personality assessment and your own self-assessment above. Are you a judging, perceptive, or combination type? Can you give examples of how it affects your social life, school, or work? Write a paragraph about this preference.

**4**

"Knowing thyself is the height of wisdom."
SOCRATES

# Activity

## Summarize Your Results

Look at your results above and summarize them on this composite chart. Notice that we are all unique, according to where the Xs fall on the scale.

Extravert (E) _____|_____ Introvert (I)

Sensing (S) _____|_____ Intuitive (N)

Thinking (T) _____|_____ Feeling (F)

Judging (J) _____|_____ Perceptive (P)

Write the letters representing each of your preferences: _____

The above letters represent your estimated personality type based on your understanding and knowledge of self. It is a good idea to confirm that this type is correct for you by completing the TruTalent Personality assessment.

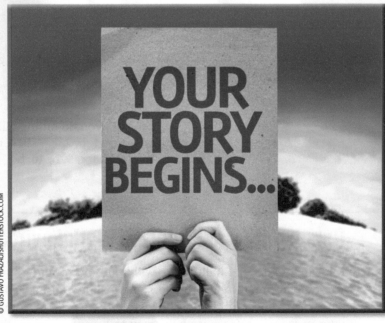

© GUSTAVO FRAZAO/SHUTTERSTOCK.COM

# Quiz

## Personality Types

Test what you have learned by selecting the correct answer to the following questions.

1. A person who is energized by social interaction is a/an:
   a. introvert
   b. extravert
   c. feeling type

2. A person who is quiet and reserved is a/an:
   a. introvert
   b. extravert
   c. perceptive type

3. A person who relies on experience and trusts information that is concrete and observable is a/an:
   a. judging type
   b. sensing type
   c. perceptive type

4. A person who focuses on "what could be" is a/an:
   a. perceptive type
   b. thinking type
   c. intuitive type

5. A person who makes decisions based on logic is a/an:
   a. thinker
   b. perceiver
   c. sensor

6. A person who makes decisions based on personal values is a/an:
   a. feeling type
   b. thinking type
   c. judging type

7. The perceptive type:
   a. has extrasensory perception
   b. likes to live life in a spontaneous and flexible way
   c. always considers feelings before making a decision

8. The judging type likes to:
   a. judge others
   b. use logic
   c. live in a structured and orderly way

9. Personality assessments are an exact predictor of your best major and career.
   a. true
   b. false

10. Some personality types are better than others.
    a. true
    b. false

**How did you do on the quiz? Check your answers: 1. b, 2. a, 3. b, 4. c, 5. a, 6. a, 7. b, 8. c, 9. b, 10. b**

# Personality and Preferred Work Environment

Knowing your personality type will help you to understand your preferred work environment and provide some insights into selecting the major and career that you would enjoy. Selecting the work environment that matches your personal preferences helps you to be energized on the job and to minimize stress. Understanding other types will help you to work effectively with coworkers. As you read this section, think about your ideal work environment and how others are different.

**Extroverts** are career generalists who use their skills in a variety of ways. Extroverts

- like variety and social interaction.
- communicate well and meet people easily.
- learn new tasks by talking with others and trying out new ideas.
- are energized by working as part of a team.

**Introverts** Introverts are career specialists who develop in-depth skills. Introverts

- prefer to focus on a task until it is complete.
- choose to work alone or with one other person.
- prefer written communication.
- are energized when they can work in a quiet environ-ment with few interruptions.

**Sensing types** are realistic and practical and like to develop standard ways of doing the job. Sensing types

- are observant and interested in facts and finding the truth.
- use common sense and learn from experience.
- keep track of details, do precise work, and like to follow routines.
- are energized when they are doing practical work with tangible outcomes.

**Intuitive types** like to work on challenging and complex problems where they can follow their inspirations to find creative solutions. Intuitive types

- focus on the whole picture rather than the details.
- enjoy change and finding new ways of doing the job.
- are initiators, promoters, and inventors of ideas.
- are energized by working in an environment where they can use creative insight, imagination, originality, and individual initiative.

**Thinking types** like to use logical analysis in making decisions. Thinking types

- expect logical reasons before accepting new ideas.
- are objective and rational and treat others fairly.
- enjoy working with others who are competent and efficient.
- are energized when they are respected for their expertise and recognized for a job well done.

**Feeling types** like harmony and the support of coworkers. Feeling types

- know their personal values and apply them consistently.
- are personal, enjoy warm relationships, and relate well to most people.

- enjoy doing work that provides a service to people and contributes to humanity.
- are energized when they work in a friendly, congenial, and supportive work environment.

**Judging types** like a work environment that is structured, settled, and organized. Judging types

- make lists and get the job done on time.
- prefer work assignments that are clear and definite.
- excel at purposeful and exacting work.
- are energized by working in a predictable and orderly environment with clear responsibilities and deadlines.

**Perceptive types** like to be spontaneous and go with the flow. Perceptive types

- feel restricted by structures and schedules.
- are comfortable in handling the unplanned or unexpected work environment.
- can adapt and deal with change.
- are energized in a flexible work environment where they can relax and control their own time.

# Personality and Decision Making

The thinking and feeling dimensions of personality are the most important factors in determining how a decision is made. Of course, people use both thinking and feeling in the decision-making process but tend to trust either thinking or feeling.

**Those who prefer thinking** base their decisions on objective and impersonal criteria. Thinking types

- examine the consequences of alternative decisions.
- use laws and principles to treat everyone fairly.
- are firm minded once the decision has been made because it was based on logic.
- can be critical of those who do not base their decisions on logic.

**Those who prefer feeling** consider human values and motives in the decision-making process, whether those values and motives are logical or not. Feeling types

- value harmony and good relationships, which are important factors in a decision.
- carefully consider how the alternatives will affect other people.
- are interested in making a decision that is agreeable to all the parties.
- are tactful and skillful in dealing with people.

Good decisions are made when both thinking and feeling types collaborate. Thinking types need to know that people are important in making decisions. Feeling types need to know that behavior will have logical consequences and that they may need to keep emotions more controlled to work effectively with thinking types.

## Personality and Time Management

The judging and perceptive personality dimensions are the dimensions most connected to time management.

**Judging types** like to have things under control and live in a planned and orderly manner. Judging types

- are naturally good at time management.
- use schedules and calendars as tools for time management and organization.
- excel at meeting deadlines
- find it difficult to relax until projects are completed.

Because judging types like to have projects under control, there is a danger that projects will be completed too quickly and that quality will suffer. Judging types may need to slow down and take the time to do quality work. They may also need to make relaxation and recreation a priority to avoid excessive stress.

**Perceptive types** prefer more spontaneity and flexibility. Perceptive types

- prioritize relaxation, having fun, and participating in recreation.
- want to brainstorm ideas when working on projects and are not too concerned about completing them—there is always more information to gather and more possibilities to explore.
- are likely to procrastinate on decisions and completing projects.
- may have several projects going at once and can be easily distracted as they move from project to project.

Perceptive types may need to focus on a few projects at a time in order to complete them. They need to develop time-management skills and work on becoming more organized to complete assignments on time.

## Journal Entry

Write a paragraph about how being a judging, perceptive, or combination type influences any of the following: how you manage your time, how you budget your money, or your preferred work environment. Remember that judging means orderly and organized, not judging other people; perceptive means spontaneous and flexible. How is this information useful in choosing your career or being successful in college?

> "Choose a job you love, and you will never have to work a day in your life."
> CONFUCIUS

# Personality and Career Choice

While it is not possible to predict exactly your career and college major by knowing your personality type, it can be helpful in providing opportunities for exploration. Here are some general descriptions of personality types and preferred careers. Included are general occupational fields, frequently chosen occupations, and suggested majors. These suggestions about career selections are based on the general characteristics of each type and research that correlates personality type with choice of a satisfying career.[1] Read the descriptions, careers, and majors that match your personality type, and then continue your career exploration with the online database in the TruTalent Personality assessment included with your textbook.

# ISTJ

ISTJs are responsible, loyal, stable, practical, down-to-earth, hardworking, and reliable. They can be depended upon to follow through with tasks. They value tradition, family, and security. They are natural leaders who prefer to work alone, but can adapt to working with teams if needed. They like to be independent and have time to think things through. They are able to remember and use concrete facts and information. They make decisions by applying logic and rational thinking. They appreciate structured and orderly environments and deliver products and services in an efficient and orderly way.

## General occupations to consider

| | | |
|---|---|---|
| business | education | health care |
| service | technical | military |
| law and law enforcement | engineering | management |

## Specific job titles

| | | |
|---|---|---|
| business executive | lawyer | electronic technician |
| administrator | judge | computer occupations |
| manager | police officer | dentist |
| real estate agent | detective | pharmacist |
| accountant | corrections officer | primary care physician |
| bank employee | teacher (math, trade, | nursing administrator |
| stockbroker | technical) | respiratory therapist |
| auditor | educational administrator | physical therapist |
| hairdresser | coach | optometrist |
| cosmetologist | engineer | chemist |
| legal secretary | electrician | military officer or |
| | | enlistee |

## College majors

| | | |
|---|---|---|
| business | engineering | chemistry |
| education | computers | biology |
| mathematics | health occupations | vocational training |
| law | | |

# ISTP

ISTPs are independent, practical, and easygoing. They prefer to work individually and frequently like to work outdoors. These types like working with objects and often are good at working with their hands and mastering tools. They are interested in how and why things work and are able to apply technical knowledge to solving practical problems. Their logical thinking makes them good troubleshooters and problem solvers. They enjoy variety, new experiences, and taking risks. They prefer environments with little structure and have a talent for managing crises. The ISTP is happy with occupations that involve challenge, change, and variety.

## General occupations to consider

| | | |
|---|---|---|
| sales | technical | business and finance |
| service | health care | vocational training |
| corrections | | |

## Specific job titles

| | | |
|---|---|---|
| sales manager | engineer | office manager |
| insurance agent | electronics technician | small business manager |
| cook | software developer | banker |
| firefighter | computer programmer | economist |
| pilot | radiologic technician | legal secretary |
| race car driver | exercise physiologist | paralegal |
| police officer | coach | computer repair |
| corrections officer | athlete | airline mechanic |
| judge | dental assistant/hygienist | carpenter |
| attorney | physician | construction worker |
| intelligence agent | optometrist | farmer |
| detective | physical therapist | military officer or enlistee |

## College majors

| | | |
|---|---|---|
| business | computers | health occupations |
| vocational training | biology | physical education |
| law | | |

# ISFJ

**ISFJs** are quiet, friendly, responsible, hardworking, productive, devoted, accurate, thorough, and careful. They value security, stability, and harmony. They like to focus on one person or project at a time. ISFJs prefer to work with individuals and are very skillful in understanding people and their needs. They often provide service to others in a very structured way. They are careful observers, remember facts, and work on projects requiring accuracy and attention to detail. They have a sense of space and function that leads to artistic endeavors such as interior decorating or landscaping. ISFJs are most comfortable working in environments that are orderly, structured, and traditional. While they often work quietly behind the scenes, they like their contributions to be recognized and appreciated.

## General occupations to consider

| | | |
|---|---|---|
| health care | education | artistic |
| social service | business | religious occupations |
| corrections | technical | vocational training |

## Specific job titles

| | | |
|---|---|---|
| nurse | social worker | counselor |
| physician | social services | secretary |
| medical technologist | administrator | cashier |
| dental hygienist | child care worker | accountant |
| health education | speech pathologist | personnel administrator |
| practitioner | librarian | credit counselor |
| dietician | curator | business manager |
| physical therapist | genealogist | paralegal |
| nursing educator | corrections worker | computer occupations |
| health administrator | probation officer | engineer |
| medical secretary | teacher (preschool, | interior decorator |
| dentist | grades 1–12) | home economist |
| medical assistant | guidance counselor | religious educator |
| optometrist | educational administrator | clergy |
| occupational therapist | | |

## College majors

| | | |
|---|---|---|
| health occupations | education | graphics |
| biology | business | religious studies |
| psychology | engineering | vocational training |
| sociology | art | |

# ISFP

**ISFPs** are quiet, reserved, trusting, loyal, committed, sensitive, kind, creative, and artistic. They have an appreciation for life and value serenity and aesthetic beauty. These types are individualistic and generally have no desire to lead or follow; they prefer to work independently. They have a keen awareness of their environment and often have a special bond with children and animals. ISFPs are service-oriented and like to help others. They like to be original and unconventional. They dislike rules and structure and need space and freedom to do things in their own way.

## General occupations to consider

| | | |
|---|---|---|
| artists | technical | business |
| health care | service | vocational training |

## Specific job titles

| | | |
|---|---|---|
| artist | recreation services | forester |
| designer | physical therapist | botanist |
| fashion designer | radiologic technician | geologist |
| jeweler | medical assistant | mechanic |
| gardener | dental assistant/hygienist | marine biologist |
| potter | veterinary assistant | teacher (science, art) |

| | | |
|---|---|---|
| painter | veterinarian | police officer |
| dancer | animal groomer/trainer | beautician |
| landscape designer | dietician | merchandise planner |
| carpenter | optician/optometrist | stock clerk |
| electrician | exercise physiologist | store keeper |
| engineer | occupational therapist | counselor |
| chef | art therapist | social worker |
| nurse | pharmacy technician | legal secretary |
| counselor | respiratory therapist | paralegal |

## College majors

| | | |
|---|---|---|
| art | forestry | psychology |
| health occupations | geology | counseling |
| engineering | education | social work |
| physical education | business | vocational training |
| biology | | |

# INFJ

**INFJs** are idealistic, complex, compassionate, authentic, creative, and vision-ary. They have strong value systems and search for meaning and purpose to life. Because of their strong value systems, INFJs are natural leaders or at least follow those with similar ideas. They intuitively understand people and ideas and come up with new ideas to provide service to others. These types like to organize their time and be in control of their work.

## General occupations to consider

| | | |
|---|---|---|
| counseling | religious occupations | health care |
| education | creative occupations | social services |
| science | arts | business |

## Specific job titles

| | | |
|---|---|---|
| career counselor | director of religious | dental hygienist |
| psychologist | education | speech pathologist |
| teacher (high school or | fine artist | nursing educator |
| college English, art, | playwright | medical secretary |
| music, social sciences, | novelist | pharmacist |
| drama, foreign | poet | occupational therapist |
| languages, health) | designer | human resources |
| librarian | architect | manager |
| home economist | art director | marketer |
| social worker | health care administrator | employee assistance |
| clergy | physician | program |
| | biologist | merchandise planner |
| | | environmental lawyer |

## College majors

| | | |
|---|---|---|
| psychology | drama | architecture |
| counseling | foreign languages | biology |
| education | English | business |
| art | health occupations | law |
| music | social work | science |

# INFP

INFPs are loyal, devoted, sensitive, creative, inspirational, flexible, easygoing, complex, and authentic. They are original and individualistic and prefer to work alone or with other caring and supportive individuals. These types are service-oriented and interested in personal growth. They develop deep relationships because they understand people and are genuinely interested in them. They dislike dealing with details and routine work. They prefer a flexible working environment with a minimum of rules and regulations.

## General occupations to consider

| | | |
|---|---|---|
| creative arts | counseling | health care |
| education | religious occupations | organizational development |

## Specific job titles

| | | |
|---|---|---|
| artist | photographer | dietician |
| designer | carpenter | psychiatrist |
| writer | teacher (art, drama, | physical therapist |
| journalist | music, English, foreign | occupational therapist |
| entertainer | languages) | speech pathologist |
| architect | psychologist | laboratory technologist |
| actor | counselor | public health nurse |
| editor | social worker | dental hygienist |
| reporter | librarian | physician |
| journalist | clergy | human resources |
| musician | religious educator | specialist |
| graphic designer | missionary | social scientist |
| art director | church worker | consultant |

## College majors

| | | |
|---|---|---|
| art | foreign languages | medicine |
| music | architecture | health occupations |
| graphic design | education | social work |
| journalism | religious studies | counseling |
| English | psychology | business |

# INTJ

**INTJs** are reserved, detached, analytical, logical, rational, original, independent, creative, ingenious, innovative, and resourceful. They prefer to work alone and work best alone. They can work with others if their ideas and competence are respected. They value knowledge and efficiency. They enjoy creative and intellectual challenges and understand complex theories. They create order and structure. They prefer to work with autonomy and control over their work. They dislike factual and routine kinds of work.

## General occupations to consider

| | | |
|---|---|---|
| business and finance | education | law |
| technical occupations | health care and medicine | creative occupations |
| science | architecture | engineering |

## Specific job titles

| | | |
|---|---|---|
| management consultant | astronomer | dentist |
| human resources planner | computer programmer | biomedical engineer |
| economist | biomedical researcher | attorney |
| international banker | software developer | manager |
| financial planner | network integration | judge |
| investment banker | specialist | electrical engineer |
| scientist | teacher (university) | writer |
| scientific researcher | school principal | journalist |
| chemist | mathematician | artist |
| biologist | psychiatrist | inventor |
| computer systems analyst | psychologist | architect |
| electronic technician | neurologist | actor |
| design engineer | physician | musician |
| architect | | |

## College majors

| | | |
|---|---|---|
| business | physics | journalism |
| finance | education | art |
| chemistry | mathematics | architecture |
| biology | medicine | drama |
| computers | psychology | music |
| engineering | law | vocational training |
| astronomy | English | |

# INTP

**INTPs** are logical, analytical, independent, original, creative, and insightful. They are often brilliant and ingenious. They work best alone and need quiet time to concentrate. They focus their attention on ideas and are frequently detached from other people. They love theory and abstract ideas and value knowledge and competency. INTPs are creative thinkers who are not too interested in practical application. They dislike detail and routine and need freedom to develop, analyze, and critique new ideas. These types maintain high standards in their work.

## General occupations to consider

| | | |
|---|---|---|
| planning and development | technical professional | academic creative occupations |
| health care | | |

## Specific job titles

| | | |
|---|---|---|
| computer software designer | pharmacist | historian |
| computer programmer | engineer | philosopher |
| research and development | electrician | college teacher |
| systems analyst | dentist | researcher |
| financial planner | veterinarian | logician |
| investment banker | lawyer | photographer |
| physicist | economist | creative writer |
| plastic surgeon | psychologist | artist |
| psychiatrist | architect | actor |
| chemist | psychiatrist | entertainer |
| biologist | mathematician | musician |
| pharmaceutical researcher | archaeologist | inventor |

## College majors

| | | |
|---|---|---|
| computers | philosophy | mathematics |
| business | music | archaeology |
| physics | art | history |
| chemistry | drama | English |
| biology | engineering | drama |
| astronomy | psychology | music |
| medicine | architecture | vocational training |

# ESTP

**ESTPs** have great people skills and are action-oriented, fun, flexible, adaptable, and resourceful. They enjoy new experiences and dealing with people. They remember facts easily and have excellent powers of observation that they use to analyze other people. They are good problem solvers and can react quickly in an emergency. They like adventure and risk and are alert to new opportunities. They start new projects but do not necessarily follow through to completion. They prefer environments without too many rules and restrictions.

## General occupations to consider

| | | |
|---|---|---|
| sales | entertainment | technical |
| service | sports | trade |
| active careers | health care | business |
| finance | | |

## Specific job titles

| | | |
|---|---|---|
| marketing professional | insurance agent | dentist |
| firefighter | sportscaster | carpenter |
| police officer | news reporter | farmer |
| corrections officer | journalist | construction worker |
| paramedic | tour agent | electrician |
| detective | dancer | teacher (trade, industrial, |
| pilot | bartender | technical) |
| investigator | auctioneer | chef |
| real estate agent | professional athlete or | engineer |
| exercise physiologist | coach | surveyor |
| flight attendant | fitness instructor | radiologic technician |
| sports merchandise sales | recreation leader | entrepreneur |
| stockbroker | optometrist | land developer |
| financial planner | pharmacist | retail sales |
| investor | critical care nurse | car sales |

## College majors

| | | |
|---|---|---|
| business | vocational training | English |
| physical education | education | journalism |
| health occupations | | |

# ESTJ

**ESTJs** are loyal, hardworking, dependable, thorough, practical, realistic, and energetic. They value security and tradition. Because they enjoy working with people and are orderly and organized, these types like to take charge and be the leader. This personality type is often found in administrative and management positions. ESTJs work systematically and efficiently to get the job done. These types are fair, logical, and consistent. They prefer a stable and predictable environment filled with action and a variety of people.

## General occupations to consider

| | | |
|---|---|---|
| managerial | service | professional |
| sales | technical | military leaders |
| business | agriculture | |

## Specific job titles

| | | |
|---|---|---|
| retail store manager | military officer or enlistee | physician |
| fire department manager | office manager | chemical engineer |
| small business manager | purchasing agent | auditor |
| restaurant manager | police officer | coach |
| financial or bank officer | factory supervisor | public relations worker |
| school principal | corrections | cook |
| sales manager | insurance agent | personnel or labor |
| top-level manager in city/ | detective |    relations worker |
|    county/state | judge | teacher (trade, |
|    government | accountant |    industrial, technical) |
| management consultant | nursing administrator | mortgage banker |
| corporate executive | mechanical engineer | |

## College majors

| | | |
|---|---|---|
| business | small business | law |
| business management |    management | education |
| accounting | engineering | vocational training |
| finance | agriculture | |

# ESFP

**ESFPs** are practical, realistic, independent, fun, social, spontaneous, and flexible. They have great people skills and enjoy working in environments that are friendly, relaxed, and varied. They know how to have a good time and make an environment fun for others. ESFPs have a strong sense of aesthetics and are sometimes artistic and creative. They often have a special bond with people or animals. They dislike structure and routine. These types can handle many activities or projects at once.

## General occupations to consider

| | | |
|---|---|---|
| education | health care | business and sales |
| social service | entertainment | service |
| food preparation | child care | |

## Specific job titles

| | | |
|---|---|---|
| child care worker | medical assistant | promoter |
| teacher (preschool, | critical care nurse | special events coordinator |
|    elementary school, | dentist | editor or reporter |
|    foreign languages, | dental assistant | retail merchandiser |
|    mathematics) | exercise physiologist | fund raiser |
| athletic coach | dog obedience trainer | receptionist |
| counselor | veterinary assistant | real estate agent |

library assistant
police officer
public health nurse

travel or tour agent
recreation leader or
   amusement site
   worker

insurance agent
sporting equipment sales
   retail sales

respiratory therapist
physical therapist
physician
emergency medical
   technician
dental hygienist
chef

photographer
designer
film producer
musician
performer
actor

retail management
waiter or waitress
cashier
cosmetologist
hairdresser
religious worker

## College majors

education
psychology
foreign languages
mathematics
physical education
culinary arts

health occupations
art
design
photography
English
child development

journalism
drama
music
business
vocational training

# ESFJ

**ESFJs** are friendly, organized, hardworking, productive, conscientious, loyal, dependable, and practical. These types value harmony, stability, and security. They enjoy interacting with people and receive satisfaction from giving to others. ESFJs enjoy working in a cooperative environment in which people get along well with each other. They create order, structure, and schedules and can be depended on to complete the task at hand. They prefer to organize and control their work.

## General occupations to consider

health care
education
child care

social service
counseling

business
human resources

## Specific job titles

medical or dental assistant
nurse
radiologic technician
dental hygienist
speech pathologist
occupational therapist
dentist
optometrist
dietician

coach
administrator of
   elementary
   or secondary school
administrator of student
   personnel
child care provider
home economist
social worker

sales representative
hairdresser
cosmetologist
restaurant worker
recreation or amusement
   site worker
receptionist
office manager
cashier

pharmacist
physician
physical therapist
health education
   practitioner
medical secretary
teacher (grades 1–12,
   foreign languages,
   reading)

administrator of social
   services
police officer
counselor
community welfare
   worker
religious educator
clergy

bank employee
bookkeeper
accountant
sales
insurance agent
credit counselor
merchandise planner

## College majors

health occupations
biology
foreign languages
English

education
psychology
counseling
sociology

religious studies
business
vocational training
child development

# ENFP

**ENFPs** are friendly, creative, energetic, enthusiastic, innovative, adventurous, and fun. They have great people skills and enjoy providing service to others. They are intuitive and perceptive about people. ENFPs are good at anything that interests them and can enter a variety of fields. These types dislike routine and detailed tasks and may have difficulty following through and completing tasks. They enjoy occupations in which they can be creative and interact with people. They like a friendly and relaxed environment in which they are free to follow their inspiration and participate in adventures.

## General occupations to consider

creative occupations
marketing
business
education
environmental science

counseling
health care

religious services

social service
entrepreneurial

arts

## Specific job titles

journalist
musician
actor
entertainer
fine artist
playwright
newscaster
reporter
interior decorator
cartoonist

public relations
counselor
clergy
psychologist
teacher (health, special
   education, English, art,
   drama, music)
social worker
dental hygienist
nurse

physical therapist
consultant
inventor
sales
human resources
   manager
conference planner
employment development
   specialist
restaurateur

| graphic designer | dietician | merchandise planner |
| marketing | holistic health practitioner | environmental attorney |
| advertising | environmentalist | lawyer |

## College majors

| journalism | business (advertising, | religious studies |
| English | marketing, public | health occupations |
| drama | relations) | law |
| art | counseling | vocational training |
| graphic design | psychology | |

# ENFJ

**ENFJs** are friendly, sociable, empathetic, loyal, creative, imaginative, and responsible. They have great people skills and are interested in working with people and providing service to them. They are good at building harmony and cooperation and respect other people's opinions. These types can find creative solutions to problems. They are natural leaders who can make good decisions. They prefer an environment that is organized and structured and enjoy working as part of a team with other creative and caring people.

## General occupations to consider

| religious occupations | counseling | health care |
| creative occupations | education | business |
| communications | human services | administration |

## Specific job titles

| director of religious | newscaster | social worker |
| education | politician | home economist |
| minister | editor | nutritionist |
| clergy | crisis counselor | speech pathologist |
| public relations | school counselor | occupational therapist |
| marketing | vocational or career | physical therapist |
| writer | counselor | optometrist |
| librarian | psychologist | dental hygienist |
| journalist | alcohol and drug | family practice |
| physician | | |
| fine artist | counselor | psychiatrist |
| designer | teacher (health, art, | nursing educator |
| actor | drama, English, foreign | pharmacist |
| musician or composer | languages) | human resources |
| trainer | | |
| fundraiser | child care worker | travel agent |

| | | |
|---|---|---|
| recreational director | college humanities | small business |
| executive | | |
| TV producer | professor | sales manager |

## College majors

| | | |
|---|---|---|
| religious studies | music | counseling |
| business (public relations, marketing) | journalism | sociology |
| | English | health occupations |
| art | foreign languages | business |
| graphic design | humanities | vocational training |
| drama | psychology | |

# ENTP

ENTPs are creative, ingenious, flexible, diverse, energetic, fun, motivating, logical, and outspoken. They have excellent people skills and are natural leaders, although they dislike controlling other people. They value knowledge and competence. They are lively and energetic and make good debaters and motivational speakers. They are logical and rational thinkers who can grasp complex ideas and theories. They dislike environments that are structured and rigid. These types prefer environments that allow them to engage in creative problem solving and the creation of new ideas.

## General occupations to consider

| | | |
|---|---|---|
| creative occupations | law | health care |
| politics | business | architecture |
| engineering | science | education |

## Specific job titles

| | | |
|---|---|---|
| photographer | politician | computer professional |
| marketing professional | political manager | corrections officer |
| journalist | political analyst | sales manager |
| actor | social scientist | speech pathologist |
| writer | psychiatrist | health education |
| musician or composer | psychologist | practitioner |
| editor | engineer | respiratory therapist |
| reporter | construction laborer | dental assistant |
| advertising director | research worker | medical assistant |
| radio/TV talk show host | electrician | critical care nurse |
| producer | lawyer | counselor |
| art director | judge | human resources planner |
| new business developer | corporate executive | educator |
| architect | | |

## College majors

| | | |
|---|---|---|
| art | music | political science |
| photography | business (advertising, | psychology |
| journalism | marketing, | health occupations |
| drama | management, | computers |
| English | human resources) | vocational training |
| engineering | architecture | education |
| science | | |

# ENTJ

**ENTJs** are independent, original, visionary, logical, organized, ambitious, competitive, hardworking, and direct. They are natural leaders and organizers who identify problems and create solutions for organizations. ENTJs are often in management positions. They are good planners and accomplish goals in a timely manner. These types are logical thinkers who enjoy a structured work environment where they have opportunity for advancement. They enjoy a challenging, competitive, and exciting environment in which accomplishments are recognized.

## General occupations to consider

| | | |
|---|---|---|
| business | management | science |
| finance | health care | law |

## Specific job titles

| | | |
|---|---|---|
| executive | manager in city/county/ | accountant |
| manager | state government | auditor |
| supervisor | management trainer | financial manager |
| personnel manager | school principal | real estate agent |
| sales manager | bank officer | lawyer, judge |
| marketing manager | computer systems analyst | consultant |
| human resources planner | computer professional | engineer |
| corporate executive | credit investigator | corrections, probation |
| college administrator | mortgage broker | officer |
| health administrator | stockbroker | psychologist |
| small business owner | investment banker | physician |
| retail store manager | economist | |

## College majors

| | | |
|---|---|---|
| business management | computers | engineering |
| finance | law | psychology |
| economics | medicine | vocational training |

# Other Factors in Choosing a Major

Choosing your college major is one of the most difficult and important decisions you will make during your college years. After assessing their personality types, students often come up with many different options for a major and career. Future chapters will help you to think about your interests, values, and preferred lifestyle. This information will help you to narrow down your choices.

Once you have completed a thorough self-assessment, you may still have several majors to consider. At this point, it is important to do some research on the outlook for a selected career in the future and the pay you would receive. Sometimes students are disappointed after graduation when they find there are few job opportunities in their chosen career field. Sometimes students graduate and cannot find jobs with the salary they had hoped to earn. It is important to think about the opportunities you will have in the future. If you have several options for a career you would enjoy, you may want to consider seriously the career that has the best outlook and pay.

© MARYNA PLESHKUN/SHUTTERSTOCK.COM

According to the Bureau of Labor Statistics, fields with the best outlook include health care, computers, and new "green jobs" related to preserving the environment. The top-paying careers all require math skills and include the science,

## Some Majors with the Highest Earnings for Bachelor's Degrees, 2020*[2]

Notice that the majors with the highest earnings require math, science, and/or business.

| College Major | Beginning Median Salary | Mid-Career Median Salary |
|---|---|---|
| Petroleum Engineering | 92,300 | 182,000 |
| Electrical Engineering and Computer Science | 101,200 | 152,300 |
| Applied Economics and Management | 60,900 | 139,600 |
| Public Accounting | 60,000 | 138,800 |
| Chemical Engineering and Materials Science | 74,500 | 137,800 |
| Aeronautics and Astronautics | 74,000 | 133,100 |
| Actuarial Mathematics | 61,900 | 130,500 |
| Information and Computer Science | 70,300 | 127,600 |
| Economics and Mathematics | 65,000 | 121,400 |
| Bioengineering | 67,400 | 115,000 |
| Statistics | 63,7000 | 114,400 |
| Physics | 62,300 | 113,800 |
| Physician's Assistant | 92,900 | 112,200 |
| Environmental Health and Safety | 58,300 | 104,200 |

*Includes bachelor's degrees only. Excludes medicine, law, and careers requiring advanced degrees.

## Other Common Majors and Earnings[3]

| College Major | Beginning Median Salary | Mid-Career Median Salary |
|---|---|---|
| Business Finance | 54,600 | 99,800 |
| Accounting and Auditing | 55,400 | 95,700 |
| Entrepreneurship | 52,300 | 95,600 |
| Advertising Design | 49,300 | 89,700 |
| Biological Sciences | 46,200 | 89,200 |
| Political Science/Public Law | 43,900 | 88,900 |
| Marketing and Communications | 46,600 | 88,700 |
| Architecture | 48,300 | 87,800 |
| Construction Technology | 55,500 | 85,300 |
| Film Studies | 42,500 | 82,300 |
| Nursing | 63,700 | 80,900 |
| History | 45,300 | 80,300 |
| Literature | 44,400 | 79,500 |
| Foreign Languages | 47,800 | 78,300 |
| Web Development | 54,100 | 78,300 |
| Speech Communication | 43,900 | 76,800 |
| Forestry | 44,700 | 75,400 |
| English Language | 42,100 | 74,500 |
| Liberal Arts | 42,500 | 73,000 |
| Exercise Physiology | 41,600 | 71,701 |
| Criminal Justice | 43,700 | 71,600 |
| Art History | 44,400 | 71,200 |
| Psychology | 42,000 | 70,700 |
| Secondary Education | 42,700 | 68,500 |
| Art | 40,600 | 63,000 |

"We act as though comfort and luxury were the chief requirements of life, when all that we need to make us really happy is something to be enthusiastic about."

CHARLES KINGSLEY

engineering, computer science, health care, and business fields. Only four percent of college graduates choose the engineering and computer science fields. Since there are fewer students in these majors, the salaries are higher. If you have a talent or interest in math, you can develop this skill and use it in high-paying careers.

## Most Meaningful College Majors[4]

Money is often not the most important consideration in choosing a major. These careers were determined to be the most meaningful, with the potential for changing the world.

| College Major | Beginning Median Salary | Mid-Career Median Salary |
|---|---|---|
| Occupational Therapy | 55,100 | 89,200 |
| Physical Therapy | 53,500 | 93,900 |
| Special Education | 27,600 | 39,100 |
| Pastoral Ministry | 37,300 | 55,600 |
| Veterinary Technology | 30,600 | 41,000 |
| Respiratory Therapy | 48,200 | 63,000 |
| Mental Health | 28,100 | 38,500 |
| Fire Technology | 42,500 | 72,700 |
| Early Childhood Education | 34,100 | 43,300 |
| Social Work | 36,600 | 51,600 |
| Radiology | 49,000 | 63,400 |
| Athletic Training | 39,700 | 57,000 |
| Elementary Teaching | 34,400 | 50,700 |
| Child Development | 35,500 | 49,100 |
| Health | 41,900 | 66,400 |
| Exercise Science | 38,900 | 61,300 |
| Foods and Nutrition | 45,000 | 64,400 |

Every career counselor can tell stories about students who ask, "What is the career that makes the most money? That's the career I want!" However, if you choose a career based on money alone, you might find it difficult and uninteresting for a lifetime of work. You might even find yourself retraining later in life for a job that you really enjoy. Remember that the first step is to figure out who you are and what you like. Then look at career outlook and opportunity. If you find your passion in a career that is in demand and pays well, you will probably be very happy with your career choice. If you find your passion in a career that offers few jobs and does not pay well, you will have to use your ingenuity to find a job and make a living. Many students happily make this informed choice and find a way to make it work.

© AZINDIANLANY/SHUTTERSTOCK.COM

> "Only passions, great passions, can elevate the soul to great things."
>
> DENIS DIDEROT

## Keys to Success

### Find Your Passion

Mark Twain said, "The secret of success is making your vocation your vacation." Find what you like to do. Better yet, find your passion. If you can find your passion, it is easy to invest the time and effort necessary to be successful. Aviator Charles Lindbergh said, "It is the greatest shot of adrenaline to be doing what you've wanted to do so badly. You almost feel like you could fly without the plane."[5] We may not be as excited about our careers as Charles Lindbergh, but we can find careers that match our personalities and talents and provide meaning to our lives.

How do you know when you have found your passion? You have found your passion when you are doing an activity and you do not notice that the time is passing. The great painter Picasso often talked about how quickly time passed while he was painting. He said, "When I work, I relax; doing nothing or entertaining visitors makes me tired." Whether you are an artist, an athlete, a scientist, or a business entrepreneur, passion provides the energy needed to be successful. It helps you to grow and create. When you are using your talents to grow and create, you can find meaning and happiness in your life.

Psychologist Martin Seligman has written a book entitled *Authentic Happiness,* in which he writes about three types of work orientation: a job, a career, and a calling.[6] A job is what you do for the paycheck at the end of the week. Many college students have jobs to earn money for college. A career has deeper personal meaning. It involves achievement, prestige, and power. A calling is defined as "a passionate commitment to work for its own sake."[7] When you have found your calling, the job itself is the reward. He notes that people who have found their calling are consistently happier than those who have a job or even a career. One of the ways that you know you have found your calling is when you are in the state of "flow." The state of "flow" is defined as "complete absorption in an activity whose challenges mesh perfectly with your abilities."[8] People who experience "flow" are happier and more productive. They do not spend their days looking forward to Friday.

Understanding your personal strengths is the beginning step to finding your calling.

Seligman adds that any job can become a calling if you use your personal strengths to do the best possible job. He cited a study of hospital cleaners. Although some viewed their job as drudgery, others viewed the job as a calling. They believed that they helped patients get better by working efficiently and anticipating the needs of doctors and nurses. They rearranged furniture and decorated walls to help patients feel better. They found their calling by applying their personal talents to their jobs. As a result, their jobs became a calling.

Sometimes we wait around for passion to find us. That probably won't happen. The first step in finding your passion is to know yourself. Then find an occupation in which you can use your talents. You may be able to find your passion by looking at your present job and finding a creative way to do it based on your special talents. It has been said that there are no dead-end jobs, just people who cannot see the possibilities. Begin your search for passion by looking at your personal strengths and how you can apply them in the job market. If the job that you have now is not your passion, see what you can learn from it and then use your skills to find a career where you are more likely to find your passion.

*"Success is not the key to happiness; happiness is the key to success. If you love what you are doing, you will be successful."*

ANONYMOUS

# JOURNAL ENTRIES
## EXPLORING INTERESTS AND VALUES

Go to http://www.collegesuccess1.com/JournalEntries.htm for Word files of the Journal Entries.

## SUCCESS
## over the Internet

**Visit the *College Success Website* at http://www.collegesuccess1. com/**

The *College Success Website* is continually updated with new topics and links to the material presented in this chapter. Topics include:

- Personality profiles
- Online personality assessments
- Personality types of famous people in history
- Personality types and relationships
- Personality types and marriage
- Personality and careers
- Personality and communication
- Choosing your major
- Topics just for fun

Contact your instructor if you have any problems in accessing the *College Success Website.*

# Notes

1. Allen L. Hammer and Gerald P. Macdaid, *MBTI Career Report Manual* (CA: Consulting Psychologist Press, 1998), 57–89.
2. Payscale, "College Salary Report 2020," from https://www.payscale.com/col-lege-salary-report/majors-that-pay-you-back/bachelors, accessed January 2021.
3. Ibid.
4. Ibid.
5. Quoted in Rob Gilbert, ed., *Bits and Pieces,* December 2, 1999.
6. Martin Seligman, *Authentic Happiness* (Free Press, 2002).
7. Martin Seligman, as reported by Geoffrey Cowley, "The Science of Happiness," *Newsweek,* September 16, 2002, 49.
8. Ibid.

# PERSONALITY PREFERENCES

Use the textbook and personality assessment to think about your personality type. Place an X on the scale to show your degree of preference for each dimension of personality.

Introvert _____ Extravert

Sensing _____ INtuitive

Thinking _____ Feeling

Judging _____ Perceptive

Write a key word or phrase to describe each preference.

Introvert

Extravert

Sensing

INtuitive

Thinking

Feeling

Judging

Perceptive

What careers are suggested by your personality assessment?

Was the personality assessment accurate and useful to you?

# PERSONALITY SCENARIOS

Read the chapter on personality before commenting on these scenarios. Keep in mind the theory that we are all born with certain personality types and there are no good or bad types. Each type has gifts and talents that can be used to be a successful and happy person. Relate your comments to the concepts in this chapter. Your instructor may have you do this exercise as a group activity in class.

Scenario 1 (Sensing vs. Intuitive): Julie is a preschool teacher. She assigns her class to draw a picture of a bicycle. Students share their pictures with the class. One of the students has drawn a bicycle with wings. Another student laughs at the drawing and says, "Bicycles don't have wings!" How should the teacher handle this situation?

Scenario 2 (Thinking vs. Feeling): John has the almost perfect girlfriend. She is beautiful, intelligent, and fun to be with. She only has one flaw: John thinks that she is too emotional and wishes she could be a little more rational. When his girlfriend tries to talk to him about emotional issues, he analyzes her problems and proposes a logical solution. His girlfriend doesn't like the solutions that John proposes. Should John find a new girlfriend?

Scenario 3 (Introvert vs. Extravert): Mary is the mother of two children, ages five (daughter) and eight (son). The five-year-old is very social and especially enjoys birthday parties. At the last party, she invited 24 girls and they all showed up at the party. Everyone had a great time. The eight-year-old is very quiet and spends his time reading, doing artwork, building models, and hanging out with his one best friend. Mary is concerned that her son does not have very many friends. She decides to have a birthday party for her son also. The only problem is that he cannot come up with a list of children to invite to the party. What should Mary do?

Scenario 4 (Judging vs. Perceptive): Jerry and Jennifer have just been married, and they love each other very much. Jennifer likes to keep the house neat and orderly and likes to plan out activities so that there are no surprises. Jerry likes creative disorder. He leaves his things all over the house. He often comes up with creative ideas for having fun. How can Jerry and Jennifer keep their good relationship going?

# TALKERS AND LISTENERS

In the classroom, talkers (extroverts) volunteer to speak and do so frequently. Listeners (introverts) are people who prefer to stay quiet and rarely join in on the discussions. Even though you may prefer talking or listening, it is best to develop both of these skills. Decide whether you are generally a talker or a listener and answer the following questions. Your instructor may want to do this as a group activity in the classroom.

## Talkers

1.  What made me a talker?

2.  How can I develop my listening skills?

3.  How can I help listeners talk more?

## Listeners

1.  What made me a listener?

2.  How can I develop my talking skills?

3.  How can I help talkers listen more?

# Exploring Interests and Values

# 3

## Learning

### OBJECTIVES

Read to answer these key questions:

- What are my interests?

- What lifestyle do I prefer?

- How do my interests relate to possible careers?

- What are my values?

- How do I put my values into action?

**Holland's Basic Categories of Career Interests**

- Realistic
- Investigative
- Artistic
- Social
- Enterprising
- Conventional

Becoming aware of your interests and values will increase self-understanding and help you to make good decisions about your college major and future career. Interests and values are also important considerations in thinking about your preferred lifestyle.

# Exploring Your Interests

Interests are simply what a person likes to do. Interests are a result of many factors, including personality, family life, values, and the environment. Knowing about your interests is helpful in planning a satisfying career. By studying people who are satisfied with their careers, psychologists have been able to help people choose careers based on their interests.

The U.S. Department of Labor has developed the O*Net Interest Profiler, which helps to identify your career interests.[1] The O*Net Interest Profiler is compatible with Holland's Theory of Vocational Personality. This is one of the most widely accepted approaches to vocational choice. According to the theory, there are six vocational personality types. These six types and their accompanying definitions are presented below.[2] As you read through each description, think about your own interests.

## Realistic

People with **realistic** interests like work activities that include practical, hands-on problems and solutions. They enjoy dealing with plants, animals, and real-world materials like wood, tools, and machinery. They enjoy outside work. Often people with realistic interests do not like occupations that mainly involve doing paperwork or working closely with others.

## Investigative

People with **investigative** interests like work activities that have to do with ideas and thinking more than with physical activity. They like to search for facts and figure out problems mentally rather than to persuade or lead people.

## Artistic

People with **artistic** interests like work activities that deal with the artistic side of things, such as forms, designs, and patterns. They like self-expression in their work. They prefer settings where work can be done without following a clear set of rules.

# Social

People with **social** interests like work activities that assist others and promote learning and personal development. They prefer to communicate more than to work with objects, machines, or data. They like to teach, give advice, help, or otherwise be of service to people.

# Enterprising

People with **enterprising** interests like work activities that have to do with starting up and carrying out projects, especially business ventures. They like persuading and leading people and making decisions. They like taking risks for profit. These people prefer action rather than thought.

# Conventional

People with **conventional** interests like work activities that follow set procedures and routines. They prefer working with data and detail rather than with ideas. They prefer work in which there are precise standards rather than work in which you have to judge things by yourself. These people like working where the lines of authority are clear.

"Even if you're on the right track, you'll get run over if you just sit there."
WILL ROGERS

According to Holland, most individuals can be described by one or more of these six personality types, frequently summarized as R-I-A-S-E-C (the first letter of each personality type). Additionally, the theory proposes that there are six corresponding work environments (or occupational groups), and that people seek out work environments that match their personality types. The better the match individuals make, the more satisfied they will be with their jobs.[3]

Holland arranged these interests on a hexagon that shows the relationship of the interests to one another. He notes that most people are not just one type, but rather a combination of types. Types that are close to each other on the hexagon are likely to have interests in common. For example, a person who is social is likely to have some artistic interests and some enterprising interests. Interests on opposite points of the hexagon are very different. For example, artistic and conventional types are opposites. Artistic types prefer freedom to be creative; conventional types prefer structure and order. The figure that follows illustrates the relationship between interest areas.[4]

"Real success is finding your life work in work that you love."
DAVID MCCULLOUGH

**FIGURE 3.1  Relationships between interest areas.**

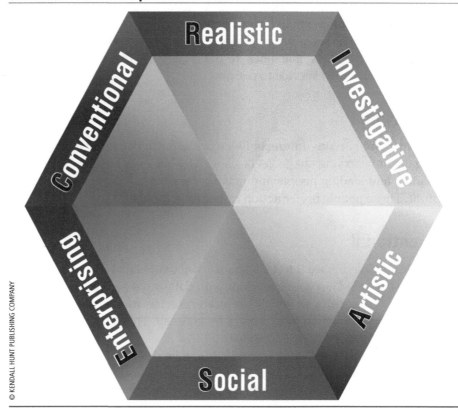

# Activity

## The Interest Profiler[5]

Place a checkmark next to the items in each list that you might **like to do**. Keep a positive attitude when thinking about your interests. You do not need to know how to do these activities or have the opportunity to do them to select items that you might like to do in the future. Also, be careful not to select an activity just because it is likely to produce higher income. You can earn higher income by increasing your skills and education in these areas. For example, if you would like to build a brick walkway, you could work in construction, or with more education, become a civil engineer. Just indicate what you would enjoy doing. Remember that this is not a test and that there are no right or wrong answers to the questions. The goal is for you to learn more about your personal career interests and related occupations.

When you are finished with each section, tally the number of checkmarks in each area. Sample job titles for each area of interest are included. Underline any jobs that appeal to you. You can also match your interests to over 900 occupations listed at http://www.onetonline.org/find/descriptor/browse/Interests/. This site includes information on specific occupations, including work tasks; tools and technology; knowledge, skills, and abilities required; work activities and work context; level of education required; work styles; work values; and wages and employment information.

## Realistic (R)

I would like to:

| | |
|---|---|
| _____ Build kitchen cabinets | _____ Assemble products in a factory |
| _____ Guard money in an armored car | _____ Catch fish as a member of a fishing crew |
| _____ Operate a dairy farm | _____ Refinish furniture |
| _____ Lay brick or tile | _____ Fix a broken faucet |
| _____ Monitor a machine on an assembly line | _____ Do cleaning or maintenance work |
| _____ Repair household appliances | _____ Maintain the grounds of a park |
| _____ Drive a taxi cab | _____ Operate a machine on a production line |
| _____ Install flooring in houses | _____ Spray trees to prevent the spread of harmful insects |
| _____ Raise fish in a fish hatchery | _____ Test the quality of parts before shipment |
| _____ Build a brick walkway | |
| _____ Assemble electronic parts | _____ Operate a motorboat to carry passengers |
| _____ Drive a truck to deliver packages to offices and homes | _____ Repair and install locks |
| _____ Paint houses | _____ Set up and operate machines to make products |
| _____ Enforce fish and game laws | _____ Put out forest fires |
| _____ Operate a grinding machine in a factory | |
| _____ Work on an offshore oil-drilling rig | |
| _____ Perform lawn care services | |

$$ R = \boxed{\phantom{XXXX}} $$

### Matching Job Titles for Realistic Interests[6]

Construction worker, building contractor, cook, landscaper, housekeeper, janitor, firefighter, hazardous materials removal worker, security guard, truck driver, automotive mechanic, cardiovascular technologist, civil engineer, commercial pilot, computer support specialist, plumber, police officer, chemical engineer, fish and game warden, surveyor, archaeologist, athletic trainer, dentist, veterinarian

## Investigative (I)

I would like to:

| | |
|---|---|
| _____ Study space travel | _____ Study whales and other types of marine life |
| _____ Make a map of the bottom of an ocean | _____ Investigate crimes |
| _____ Study the history of past civilizations | _____ Study the movement of planets |
| _____ Study animal behavior | _____ Examine blood samples using a microscope |

_____ Develop a new medicine

_____ Plan a research study

_____ Study ways to reduce water pollution

_____ Develop a new medical treatment or procedure

_____ Determine the infection rate of a new disease

_____ Study rocks and minerals

_____ Diagnose and treat sick animals

_____ Study the personalities of world leaders

_____ Conduct chemical experiments

_____ Conduct biological research

_____ Study the population growth of a city

_____ Investigate the cause of a fire

_____ Study the structure of the human body

_____ Develop psychological profiles of criminals

_____ Develop a way to better predict the weather

_____ Work in a biology lab

_____ Invent a replacement for sugar

_____ Study genetics

_____ Study the governments of different countries

_____ Do research on plants or animals

_____ Do laboratory tests to identify diseases

_____ Study weather conditions

I =

**Matching Job Titles for Investigative Interests**

Electronic engineering technician, emergency medical technician, fire investigator, paralegal, police detective, engineer (aerospace, biomedical, chemical, electrical, computer, environmental, or industrial), chemist, computer systems analyst, geoscientist, market research analyst, anesthesiologist, biochemist, biophysicist, clinical psychologist, dietician, physician, microbiologist, pharmacist, psychiatrist, surgeon, veterinarian, science teacher, college professor

## Artistic (A)

I would like to:

_____ Conduct a symphony orchestra

_____ Write stories or articles for magazines

_____ Direct a play

_____ Create dance routines for a show

_____ Write books or plays

_____ Play a musical instrument

_____ Perform comedy routines in front of an audience

_____ Perform as an extra in movies, plays, or television shows

_____ Write reviews of books or plays

_____ Compose or arrange music

_____ Act in a movie

_____ Dance in a Broadway show

_____ Draw pictures

_____ Sing professionally

_____ Perform stunts for a movie or television show

_____ Create special effects for movies

_____ Conduct a musical choir

_____ Act in a play

_____ Paint sets for plays

_____ Audition singers and musicians for a musical show

_____ Design sets for plays

_____ Announce a radio show

_____ Write scripts for movies or television shows

_____ Write a song

_____ Perform jazz or tap dance

_____ Direct a movie

_____ Sing in a band

_____ Design artwork for magazines

_____ Edit movies

_____ Pose for a photographer

A =

## Matching Job Titles for Artistic Interests

Model, actor, fine artist, floral designer, singer, tile setter, architectural drafter, architect, dancer, fashion designer, film and video editor, hairdresser, makeup artist, museum technician, music composer, photographer, self-enrichment education teacher, art director, broadcast news analyst, choreographer, editor, graphic designer, landscape architect, creative writer, public relations specialist, teacher (of art, drama, or music)

## Social (S)

I would like to:

_____ Teach an individual an exercise routine

_____ Perform nursing duties in a hospital

_____ Give CPR to someone who has stopped breathing

_____ Help people with personal or emotional problems

_____ Teach children how to read

_____ Work with mentally disabled children

_____ Teach an elementary school class

_____ Give career guidance to people

_____ Supervise the activities of children at a camp

_____ Help people with family-related problems

_____ Perform rehabilitation therapy

_____ Do volunteer work at a nonprofit organization

_____ Help elderly people with their daily activities

_____ Teach children how to play sports

_____ Help disabled people improve their daily living skills

_____ Teach sign language to people with hearing disabilities

_____ Help people who have problems with drugs or alcohol

_____ Help conduct a group therapy session

_____ Help families care for ill relatives

_____ Provide massage therapy to people

_____ Plan exercises for disabled patients

_____ Counsel people who have a life-threatening illness

_____ Teach disabled people work and living skills

_____ Organize activities at a recreational facility

_____ Take care of children at a day care center

_____ Organize field trips for disabled people

_____ Assist doctors in treating patients

_____ Work with juveniles on probation

_____ Provide physical therapy to people recovering from injuries

_____ Teach a high school class

S =

## Matching Job Titles for Social Interests

Host, hostess, bartender, lifeguard, food server, child care worker, home health aide, occupational therapist, occupational therapist aide, personal and home care aide, physical therapist, physical therapist aide, veterinary assistant, dental hygienist, fitness trainer, medical assistant, nanny, teacher (preschool, kindergarten, elementary, middle, or high school), registered nurse, respiratory therapist, self-enrichment education teacher, tour guide, mediator, educational administrator, health educator, park naturalist, probation officer, recreation worker, chiropractor, clergy, counseling psychologist, social worker, substance abuse counselor, physician assistant, speech and language pathologist

## Enterprising (E)

I would like to:

_____ Buy and sell stocks and bonds

_____ Manage a retail store

_____ Sell telephone and other communication equipment

_____ Operate a beauty salon or barber shop

_____ Sell merchandise over the telephone

_____ Run a stand that sells newspapers and magazines

_____ Give a presentation about a product you are selling

_____ Buy and sell land

_____ Sell compact discs at a music store

_____ Run a toy store

_____ Manage the operations of a hotel

_____ Sell houses

_____ Sell candy and popcorn at sports events

_____ Manage a supermarket

_____ Manage a department within a large company

_____ Sell a soft drink product line to stores and restaurants

_____ Sell refreshments at a movie theater

_____ Sell hair-care products to stores and salons

_____ Start your own business

_____ Negotiate business contracts

_____ Represent a client in a lawsuit

_____ Negotiate contracts for professional athletes

_____ Be responsible for the operation of a company

_____ Market a new line of clothing

_____ Sell newspaper advertisements

_____ Sell merchandise at a department store

_____ Sell automobiles

_____ Manage a clothing store

_____ Sell restaurant franchises to individuals

_____ Sell computer equipment to a store

E =

## Matching Job Titles

Cashier, food worker, customer service representative, sales worker, supervisor, gaming dealer, inspector, retail sales clerk, chef, food service manager, operations manager, real estate broker, realtor, sheriff, wholesale or retail buyer, advertiser, appraiser, construction manager, criminal investigator, financial manager, insurance sales agent, meeting and convention planner, personal financial advisor, sales engineer, judge, lawyer, business or political science teacher, educational administrator, librarian, medical health manager, treasurer, controller

## Conventional (C)

I would like to:

_____ Develop a spreadsheet using computer software

_____ Proofread records or forms

_____ Use a computer program to generate customer bills

_____ Schedule conferences for an organization

_____ Keep accounts payable/receivable for an office

_____ Load computer software into a large computer network

_____ Transfer funds between banks using a computer

_____ Organize and schedule office meetings

_____ Use a word processor to edit and format documents

_____ Operate a calculator

_____ Direct or transfer phone calls for a large organization

_____ Perform office filing tasks

_____ Compute and record statistical and other numerical data

_____ Generate the monthly payroll checks for an office

_____ Take notes during a meeting

_____ Keep shipping and receiving records

_____ Calculate the wages of employees

_____ Assist senior-level accountants in performing bookkeeping tasks

_____ Type labels for envelopes and packages

_____ Inventory supplies using a handheld computer

_____ Develop an office filing system

_____ Keep records of financial transactions for an organization

_____ Record information from customers applying for charge accounts

_____ Photocopy letters and reports

_____ Record rent payments

_____ Enter information into a database

_____ Keep inventory records

_____ Maintain employee records

_____ Stamp, sort, and distribute mail for an organization

_____ Handle customers' bank transactions

C =

### Matching Job Titles for Conventional Interests

Cashier, cook, janitor, landscaping worker, resort desk clerk, medical records technician, medical secretary, bookkeeping and accounting clerk, dental assistant, drafter, loan officer, paralegal, pharmacy technician, purchasing agent, accountant, auditor, budget analyst, city and regional planner, computer security specialist, cost estimator, credit analyst, database administrator, environmental compliance inspector, financial analyst, geophysical data technician, librarian, proofreader, computer science teacher, pharmacist, statistician, treasurer

### Summing Up Your Results

Put the number of checkmarks from each section of the Interest Profiler on the lines that follow:

____ Realistic          ____ Social

____ Investigative      ____ Enterprising

____ Artistic           ____ Conventional

What are your top three areas of interest? (Realistic, Investigative, Artistic, Social, Enterprising, Conventional?)

1. _____

2. _____

3. _____

## Journal Entry

List your top three areas of interest from the Interest Profiler (realistic, investigative, social, enterprising, or conventional). Go to http://www .onetonline.org/find/descriptor/browse/interests/ and click on your highest interests to find some matching careers. List one career and briefly describe the education required, salary, and projected growth for one of these careers. Here is an easy outline:

My top interests on the Interest Profiler are . . . .

One career that matches my interests is . . .

The education required is . . .

The median annual salary is . . .

**1**

**FIGURE 3.2  Lifestyle Triangle.[7]**

## Interests and Lifestyle

Our occupational interests determine what we study and the kinds of occupations we choose. While study and work form the basis of our lifestyle, there are other important components. What we choose to do for fun and relaxation helps us to be refreshed and keeps life interesting. Another component of a balanced lifestyle is time spent with friends and family. It is important to choose work that allows you to have the resources and time to lead a balanced lifestyle with all of these components. A balanced lifestyle has been described as a triangle with work and study forming the base, leisure and recreation forming one side, and kinship and friendship forming the other side.

Give some thought to the kind of lifestyle you prefer. Think about balancing your work, leisure, and social activities.

## Journal
### Entry

In seeking to accomplish lifetime goals, sometimes people are not successful because they place too much emphasis on work, study, leisure, or social life. How would you balance work, study, leisure, and social life to achieve your lifetime goals?

**2**

# Quiz

## Interests

Test what you have learned by selecting the correct answers to the following questions.

1. Realistic people are likely to choose a career in
   a. construction or engineering.
   b. accounting or real estate.
   c. financial investments or banking.

2. Investigative people are likely to choose a career in
   a. art or music.
   b. teaching or social work.
   c. science or laboratory work.

3. Enterprising people are likely to choose a career in
   a. computer programming or accounting.
   b. business management or government.
   c. health care or social services.

4. Conventional people are likely to choose a career in
   a. health care or social services.
   b. financial investments or banking.
   c. manufacturing or transportation.

5. Social types generally
   a. enjoy working with tools and machines.
   b. are humanistic and idealistic.
   c. have skills in selling and communication.

**How did you do on the quiz? Check your answers: 1. a, 2. c, 3. b, 4. b, 5. b**

# Using Values to Make Important Life Decisions

Values are what we think is important and what we feel is right and good. Values come from many sources, including our parents, friends, the media, our religious background, our culture, our society, and the historical time in which we live. Our values make us different and unique individuals. Knowing our values helps us to make good decisions about work and life. For example, consider a situation in which a person is offered a high-paying job that involves a high degree of responsibility and a lot of stress. If the person values challenge and excitement and views stress as a motivator, the chances are that it would be a good decision to take the job. If the person values peace of mind and has a difficult time coping with stress, it might be better to forgo the higher income and maintain quality of life. Making decisions consistent with our values is one of the keys to happiness and success.

Values and needs are closely related. Humanistic psychologist Abraham Maslow[8] theorized that we adopt certain values to fulfill psychological or physical needs. He described needs and values in terms of a pyramid in which needs are organized in a hierarchy arranged from the most basic to the most complex and personal. We cannot move to the next higher level until lower-level needs are met. These needs, listed in order from most basic to most complex, can be defined as follows:

- **Biological needs.** Basic needs for survival, including food, water, air, and clothing.
- **Safety needs.** Basic needs for shelter and a safe and predictable environment.
- **Love and belongingness.** Includes love, respect, and caring from our family and friends.
- **Self-esteem.** Feeling good about yourself and having confidence in your abilities.
- **Intellectual.** Having the knowledge and understanding needed for survival.
- **Aesthetic.** Having an appreciation of beauty.
- **Self-actualization.** Developing and reaching your fullest potential, enabling you to contribute to society.

**FIGURE 3.3  Maslow's Hierarchy of Needs.**

An example of a practical application of this theory is finding a solution for homeless people in society. It is easy to say that they should just go get jobs. Applying Maslow's hierarchy of needs, we would say that the first step in helping the homeless is to meet their biological needs. Before they can worry about employment, they need food, water, and clothing. Next, they need shelter so they have a safe and predictable environment. They need to know that people care about them so they can develop self-esteem. Once people have self-esteem and confidence, they can begin to be trained and educated. Once they have skills, they can become employed and enjoy the good life, appreciate beauty, and reach their potential. A person who is employed pays taxes and may do volunteer work to contribute to society.

**Self-actualization** is another word for success. It means knowing about and using your talents to fulfill your potential. It means being healthy and creative. It is being the best that you can be. Abraham Maslow said, "We may still often (if not always) expect that a new discontent and restlessness will soon develop, unless the individual is doing what he's fitted for. A musician must make music, an artist must paint, a poet must write, if he's to be ultimately at peace. What a person can be, he must be. This need we call self-actualization."[9]

We are all ultimately aiming for self-actualization. Here are some characteristics of the self-actualized person:

- Feels secure, loved, and respected, and makes a connection with others,
- Values self and others,
- Is independent,
- Can make decisions and accept responsibility,
- Appreciates other people and cares for the world,
- Is open to new ideas,
- Resists conformity,
- Has little need for status symbols,
- Is emotionally balanced,
- Is not burdened with anxiety, guilt, or shame,
- Treats others with respect,
- Feels at one with humankind,
- Has deep and caring relationships,
- Can look at life with a sense of humor,
- Is creative, passionate, and enjoys life,
- Takes time for self-renewal and relaxation,
- Has strong values and a philosophy of life.

This sounds great, but may be difficult to achieve. Remember that we are always on the road to self-actualization. Life is about growing and changing. If we do not grow and change, life becomes boring. It all begins with basic needs for survival. Once we have the basic needs for survival, we can focus on wants or desires (the possibilities). We can't have everything, so we determine what is important or what we value the most. Knowing what we value helps us to make good decisions about life goals. In setting our goals, we put values into practice. Meeting the challenges of our lives and accomplishing our goals lead to satisfaction and happiness. The process looks like this:

**FIGURE 3.4  Meeting the challenges of our lives and accomplishing our goals lead to satisfaction and happiness.**

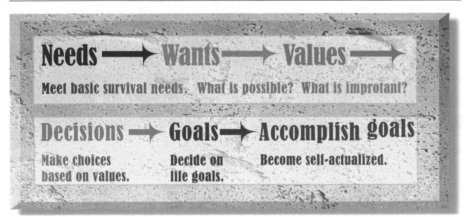

> "Try not to be a man of success, but rather to become a man of value."
> ALBERT EINSTEIN

## Journal
### Entry

Review Maslow's theory of self-actualization. How would you apply Maslow's theory to being successful in life?

**3**

## Activity

### Values Checklists

**Assessing Your Personal Values**

Use the following checklist to begin to think about what values are important to you.
Place a checkmark next to any value that is important to you. There are no right or wrong answers.
If you think of other values that are important to you, add them to the bottom of the list.

———— Having financial security

———— Making a contribution to humankind

———— Being a good parent

———— Being honest

———— Acquiring wealth

———— Being a wise person

———— Having good family relationships

———— Preserving the environment

———— Having the respect of others

———— Becoming famous

———— Happiness

———— Freedom and independence

——— Becoming an educated person

——— Believing in a higher power (God)

——— Preserving civil rights

——— Never being bored

——— Enjoying life and having fun

——— Making something out of my life

——— Being an ethical person

——— Feeling safe and secure

——— Having a good marriage

——— Having good friends

——— Having social status

——— Being patriotic

——— Having power

——— Having good morals

——— Being creative

——— Having control over my life

——— Growing and developing

——— Feeling competent

——— Feeling relaxed

——— Having prestige

——— Improving society

——— Having good mental health

——— Being a good athlete

——— Enjoying the present moment

——— Maintaining peace of mind

——— Common sense

——— Having pride in my culture

——— Doing community service

——— Achieving my goals in life

——— Having adventures

——— Having leisure time

——— Having good health

——— Being loyal

——— Having a sense of accomplishment

——— Participating in church activities

——— Being physically fit

——— Helping others

——— Being a good person

——— Having time to myself

——— Loving and being loved

——— Being physically attractive

——— Achieving something important

——— Accepting who I am

——— Appreciating natural beauty

——— Using my artistic talents

——— Feeling good about myself

——— Making a difference

——— Other: _____

——— Other: _____

——— Other: _____

## Journal Entry

What is your most important value? Why is it important to you?

**4**

# Quiz

## Values

1. To make a good decision, it is important to be aware of your values. Values describe
   a. how you spend your money.
   b. what you think is important.
   c. the best buy for your money.

2. According to Maslow, people who have reached their highest potential are
   a. self-motivated.
   b. famous.
   c. self-actualized.

3. According to Maslow, homeless people would have difficulty finding a job unless they
   a. had their biological and safety needs met.
   b. had a better work ethic.
   c. became self-actualized.

4. It is important to choose work that allows you to lead a balanced lifestyle that includes time for
   a. leisure, socializing, and study/work.
   b. fun, socializing, and following your own interests.
   c. work, study, and time for yourself.

5. To act on your values means to
   a. get good value for your money.
   b. treat others with respect.
   c. act in a manner consistent with your values.

**How did you do on the quiz? Check your answers: 1. b, 2. c, 3. a, 4. a, 5. c**

# Keys to Success

## Act on Your Values

Values are what are most important to you; they are your highest principles. They provide the road map to your success and happiness. You will face important turning points along life's journey. Should I go to college? What will be my major? What career will I have? Whom should I marry? What job should I take? Where shall I live? You can find good answers to these questions by being aware of your values and using them to make decisions and guide your actions. If your decisions follow your values, you can get what you want out of life.

The first step is knowing your values. You may need some time to think about your values and change them if they are not right for you. What values were you taught as a child? What values do you want to keep as an adult? Look around at people that you admire. What are their values? What values have you learned from your religion? Are these values important

to you? Ask your friends about their values and share yours. Revise and rethink your values periodically. Make sure your values are your own and not necessarily values that someone has told you were important. When you begin to think about values, you can come up with many things that are important. The key is to find out which values are most important. In this way, when you are faced with a choice, you will not be confused. You will know what is most important to you.

Knowing about values is not enough. It is important to act consistently with your values and to follow them. For example, if people value health but continue to smoke, they are saying one thing but doing another. If they value family but spend all of their time at work, they are not acting consistently with their values. As a result, they might find that their family is gone and they have lost something that is really valuable.

*"The great aim of education is not knowledge, but action."*

HERBERT SPENCER

Use your actions to question or reaffirm your values. Do you really value your health and family? If so, take action to preserve your good health and spend time with your family. It is necessary to periodically look at your patterns of behavior. Do you act out of habit or do you act according to what is important to you? Habits might need to be changed to get what you value most out of life.

In times of doubt and difficulty, your values can keep you going. If you truly value getting a college education, you can put in the effort to accomplish your goal. When you have doubts about whether you can be successful, examine your values again and remind yourself of why you are doing what you are doing. For example, if you value being an independent business entrepreneur, you will put in the effort to be successful. If you value being a good parent, you will find the patience and develop the skill to succeed. Reminding yourself of your values can help you to continue your commitment to accomplishing your goals.

By knowing your values and following them, you have a powerful tool for making decisions, taking action, and motivating yourself to be successful.

## Journal Entry

**5**

List one of your most important values. What actions are you taking to match your values?

One of my most important values is . . .

I am taking these actions to match this value:

## JOURNAL ENTRIES
## EXPLORING INTERESTS AND VALUES

Go to http://www.collegesuccess1.com/JournalEntries.htm for Word files of the Journal Entries.

## SUCCESS over the Internet

**Visit the *College Success Website* at http://www.collegesuccess1.com/**

The *College Success Website* is continually updated with new topics and links to the material presented in this chapter. Topics include:

- Occupations for realistic, investigative, artistic, social, enterprising, and conventional interests
- Holland's self-directed search
- Various self-assessments
- Being a self-actualized person

Contact your instructor if you have any problems in accessing the *College Success Website*.

# Notes

1. U.S. Department of Labor, "O*Net Interest Profiler," available at http://onetcenter.org

2. U.S. Department of Labor, "O*Net Interest Profiler User's Guide," available at http://onetcenter.org

3. John L. Holland, *Making Vocational Choices: A Theory of Vocational Personalities and Work Environments* (2nd Ed.), (Englewood Cliffs, NJ: Prentice-Hall, 1985).

4. U.S. Department of Labor, "O*Net Interest Profiler User's Guide."

5. Adapted from U.S. Department of Labor, "O*Net Interest Profiler."

6. Job titles in this section from http://www.onetonline.org/find/descriptor/browse/interests/

7. The Lifestyle Triangle adapted with permission from NTL Institute, "Urban Middle-Class Lifestyles in Transition," by Paula Jean Miller and Gideon Sjoberg, *Journal of Applied Behavioral Science* 9 (1973), nos. 2/3: 149.

8. Abraham Maslow, *Motivation and Personality* (New York: Harper and Row, 1970).

9. Maslow, *Motivation and Personality*, 91.

# VALUES IN ACTION

Knowing your values is important in order to make good decisions. Read the following scenarios and think about the values of the person described. Make a recommendation to answer the question posed in each case. You may want to do this exercise in a group with other students.

**Scenario 1:** What major should I choose? Shawn is 20 years old and has completed two years of college. He has been trying to decide whether to major in engineering or music. He has completed all of his general education requirements as well as several courses in music, math, and physics. As a child, Shawn was interested in science and dreamed of making new inventions. He always took things apart to see how they worked. Math was always easy for Shawn, and he received awards for achievement in science.

He also took part in band throughout his school years and learned to play several instruments. As a teenager, he had a garage band and became so interested in playing the piano that he spent two hours a day practicing. Shawn's dilemma was that he was becoming stressed out trying to do both majors and no longer had time to do well in both music and engineering. He also wanted to have time to get a part-time job in order to become more independent. Shawn's top five values are being independent and living on his own, having a secure future, doing interesting work, achieving something important, and being able to relax.

What are Shawn's values?

What major should Shawn consider? Why?

**Scenario 2:** Should I continue my education? Maria is a married mother of two young boys, ages five and seven, and a part-time college student. Maria and her husband, Juan, are very proud of their Mexican heritage and value their marriage and family. They both think that it is important for Maria to spend time with the children. Maria learned to speak English as a second language and has made sure that her children speak both English and Spanish. While the children are in school, Maria has been attending college part-time with the goal of becoming a teacher's aide in a class for bilingual children. She has some experience as a teacher's aide and gets a great deal of satisfaction from helping the children.

Juan works in construction, and the family has sacrificed to come up with the money to pay for Maria to attend college. Maria has struggled to earn her associate's degree and is proud of her accomplishments. She values her education and wants her children to do well in school. Now Maria is considering continuing her education to earn the bachelor's degree so that she can become a teacher. She would enjoy having her own classroom, loves working with children, and would have a higher income as a teacher than she would as a teacher's aide. Maria's husband is concerned that she will spend too much time at college and will not be home for the children. He is also relieved that Maria has finished college and plans to work part-time to supplement the family income while the children are in school.

What are Maria's values? Should Maria continue her education?

# TWENTY THINGS YOU LIKE TO DO

Your instructor may ask you to do this exercise in class. In five minutes, see if you can make a list of 20 things that you like to do. To help you with this list, think about the following questions:

- What do you like to do for fun in the summer? fall? winter? spring?
- What do you like to do with your family? friends?
- What do you like to do on vacation?
- What do you like to do on a rainy day when you are home alone?
- What do you like to do to relax?
- What kinds of physical activities do you like?
- What are your hobbies?
- What do you like to do at school? at work?

_____ 1. _____

_____ 2. _____

_____ 3. _____

_____ 4. _____

_____ 5. _____

_____ 6. _____

_____ 7. _____

_____ 8. _____

_____ 9. _____

_____ 10. _____

_____ 11. _____

_____ 12. _____

_____ 13. _____

_____ 14. _____

_____ 15. _____

_____ 16. _____

_____ 17. _____

_____ 18. _____

_____ 19. _____

_____ 20. _____

Write one or more of these symbols to the left of each item.

$       For activities that cost more than $20 each time you do them

P       For things that you do with people

I       For things that you do by yourself

T       For activities that involve working with things (e.g., gardening, crafts, working on your car)

D       For activities that involve working with data (e.g., working with your computer, doing budgeting, filing, organizing)

A       For activities that involve some physical activity

R       For activities that involve risk or adventure (e.g., car racing, skydiving, skiing)

MT      For activities that you would like to have more time to do

1–5     For the five most important activities, with 1 being most important

After labeling the items in your list, answer the following lifestyle questions.

1. Look at the number of items with a $ sign. How important is money to your lifestyle? Do you need a high-paying occupation, or could you take a job that pays less but offers great personal satisfaction?

2. Do you like to do things with people, things, or data? Can you see a pattern? Would you prefer to work with people or alone? Do you have the same preference for your leisure time?

3. Are you physically active? Do you enjoy risk and adventure?

4. Which items do you wish you had more time to do?

5. Look at the top five items that you selected. Why are they important to your lifestyle?

# LIFESTYLE TRIANGLE

Look at the items you selected in the exercise "Twenty Things You Like to Do." Separate them into the following categories and list them below.

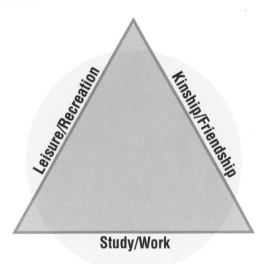

| Leisure/Recreation | Study/Work | Kinship/Friendship |
|---|---|---|
|  |  |  |

How balanced is your lifestyle? Do you need to add more activities in any of the categories?

In the future, my lifestyle will be . . .

# SUMMING UP VALUES

Look at the "Values Checklist" you completed in this chapter. Choose the 10 values most important to you and list them here.

_____     _____

_____     _____

_____     _____

_____     _____

_____     _____

Next, pick out the value that is most important and label it 1. Label your second most important value 2, and so on, until you have picked out your top five values.

1. My most important value is _____ .
   Why?

2. My second most important value is _____ .
   Why?

3. My third most important value is _____ .
   Why?

4. My fourth most important value is _____ .
   Why?




5. My fifth most important value is _____ .
   Why?

# Exploring Your Multiple Intelligences 4

## Learning
## OBJECTIVES

Read to answer these key questions:

- How does mindset affect intelligence?

- How does grit affect intelligence?

- What are multiple intelligences?

- What kinds of intelligence do I have?

- What are my personal strengths?

- What is emotional intelligence?

- How can I use the concepts of mindset and grit to accomplish my college and career goals?

Our ideas about intelligence have evolved from a single score on an intelligence test to newer theories of multiple intelligences. Older theories of intelligence assumed that it was fixed at birth and unchangeable. Newer research has shown that intelligences can be improved with effort. In this chapter, you can explore the many facets of your intelligences and think positively about your ability to improve through effort and practice.

## Your Mindset Makes a Difference

Did you know that your mindset has a powerful effect on learning and college success? Mindset is related to your self-image as a learner. It affects the effort you put into your studies and how you deal with challenges and setbacks. A positive mindset can even make you smarter as you learn new material and exercise your brain. Scientists have identified a **growth mindset** that leads to success.[1] It includes the belief that

- Intelligence is increased as you learn new knowledge.
- Through practice and effort, skills can be improved.
- Learning and self-improvement continue over a lifetime.
- Challenges are a way to be tested and improve performance.
- Failure is an opportunity to learn.
- Constructive criticism improves performance.
- The success of others is an inspiration.

In contrast, the **fixed mindset** is an obstacle to success.

It includes the following beliefs:

- Intelligence is fixed at birth.
- Increased effort does not lead to increased success.
- There is a limit to what we can accomplish.
- Roadblocks or obstacles are an excuse to be absent.
- It is best to take on only easy tasks in which success is guaranteed.
- Constructive criticism is a personal attack.
- The success of others makes me look bad.
- Hard work is unpleasant.
- The amount of work needed to be successful is underestimated.

The good news is that you can learn to identify and change your mindset so that you can be successful in college, in your career, and in your personal life. If you believe that effort can produce rewards, you are on your way to success.

> "The purpose of our lives is to give birth to the best which is within us."
> MARIANNE WILLIAMSON

## Activity: What Is Your Mindset?

Circle the number that best describes your mindset.

| | Strongly Agree | Agree | Disagree | Strongly Disagree |
|---|---|---|---|---|
| People are born with a certain amount of intelligence that cannot be changed. | 0 | 1 | 2 | 3 |
| I appreciate feedback on my performance and use it to improve my skills. | 3 | 2 | 1 | 0 |
| I avoid challenges and prefer to complete school work that is easy. | 0 | 1 | 2 | 3 |
| The more you learn, the more intelligent you become. | 3 | 2 | 1 | 0 |
| Completing challenging work is worth the effort because it gives me a sense of accomplishment. | 3 | 2 | 1 | 0 |
| When the work is difficult, I feel like I am not very smart. | 0 | 1 | 2 | 3 |
| When I receive a failing grade, I feel discouraged and feel like giving up. | 0 | 1 | 2 | 3 |
| When I receive a failing grade, I look at what I did wrong and try to do better next time. | 3 | 2 | 1 | 0 |
| I get angry when teachers or coaches tell me how to improve my performance. | 0 | 1 | 2 | 3 |
| The more work you put into learning a new skill, the better you will get at doing it. | 3 | 2 | 1 | 0 |

Write your total points here: _____

| | |
|---|---|
| 25–30 | You have a growth mindset that will help you to be successful in college. |
| 20–24 | You have many qualities of a positive mindset, but could benefit from thinking more positively about learning. |
| 15–19 | You have some qualities of a growth mindset, but would benefit from re-reading the information about growth mindset and thinking about how you can use this material to increase your success. |
| 14 or less | Re-read the material on growth mindset and think about how you can apply it to improve your success in college. |

# Grit: A Powerful Tool for Student Success

Psychologists have found that one of the most important factors related to success in college is grit. What is grit? Grit is defined as a combination of perseverance and passion. Psychologist Angela Duckworth studied students who were successful at the United States Military Academy at West Point, one of the most selective colleges in the country.[2] Even though only the top students are admitted, 20% of these students drop out before graduation. Most of the dropouts leave during the first two months of college. What is the difference between those who are successful and those who drop out? **Those who are successful have a "never give up" attitude, or grit.** They are constantly tested with tasks that challenge their skills and are successful because they have grit, and not because of superior academic or athletic ability. The successful students can keep going through challenges and even failure.

Grit includes the element of passion, or the drive to constantly improve. Successful students have a goal or vision of the future and they strive to achieve it. Their goals are achievable because they match their interests and personal strengths. For this reason, having goals that match your personal strengths and interests is essential to your success. These goals give you the motivation and grit to continue when the going gets tough. Some of you have clear goals for the future while others are re-evaluating or beginning to work on them. The material in the following chapters helps you to think about your interests and personal strengths to set goals for the future and increase the motivation to complete your education.

**What is more important, talent or grit?** We have traditionally assumed that talent or intelligence is the key to success. In fact, there is a bias in society in which people assume that success is the result of talent. We look at successful people, admire their talent, and assume that their unusual talent made them successful. However, "our talent is one thing. What we do with it is quite another."[3] The most talented individuals are not always the most successful. The great philosopher Nietzsche proposed that we think of gifted individuals as people who worked hard to become geniuses.

**How do famous people achieve excellence?** Psychologists have studied famous musicians, athletes, scientists, and others to find out what makes them successful. Rather than talent, the characteristic connected to success is **effortful training.** Effortful training involves identifying a goal that challenges your skills, finding your weaknesses, and working to improve them one small step at a time. Life is easier if you can establish a habit or daily ritual of effortful practice. For example, you can make it a habit of exercising first thing in the morning. You can make a habit of studying at a certain time and place each day. If you are in the habit of doing something, you don't have to think about it; you just do it.

It is estimated that it takes about 10,000 hours to learn a complex skill.[4] The practice is often difficult and boring, but motivated individuals persist by keeping in mind what they want to accomplish. Here are some examples of effortful practice:

- Do you want to become an NBA superstar? Superstars such as Lebron James, Giannis Antetokounmpo, Luca Doncic, and Stephen Curry spend at least five hours a day for seven days a week practicing.[5]

- Do you want to be an all pro football player? Tom Brady spends 16 hours a day practicing, viewing films, and preparing for meetings before a Super Bowl game.[6]
- Do you want to become an Olympic gold medalist gymnast? Simone Biles practices 32 hours a week, six days a week.[7]
- Do you want to become a world-famous violinist? Itzhak Perlman suggests that students spend from four to five hours of effortful practicing each day.[8]

These successful musicians and athletes have true grit and practice until their performance becomes a habit. The key idea is that learning complex skills is challenging, takes time, and is accomplished through effortful practice one small step at a time.

**How does grit apply to college students?** To be successful in college, it is important to spend a significant amount of time on your studies. A common rule is to spend two hours a week for each unit enrolled. For example, a three-unit course would require three hours a week in class and six hours outside of class reading and studying. Of course, the time required varies with the difficulty of the subject and your prior knowledge. In math courses, students may need to spend 10 hours per week studying and practicing problems to be successful. Start spending time studying from the very beginning. Remember that most dropouts happen early in the semester as students quickly realize that they are too behind to catch up.

Most importantly, don't give up! It is important to understand that college is challenging and requires a great deal of effort to be successful. Because college is difficult, there may be times that you may struggle or even

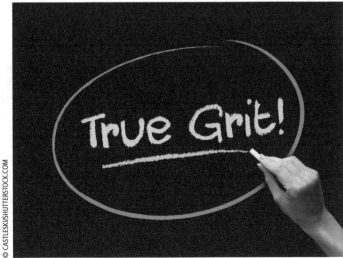

receive a failing grade. Maintain a positive attitude, spend more time on the subject, and ask for help. Seek out tutoring or see your college professor during office hours if you need extra help. Asking for help is not a sign of weakness. College professors generally respect students who are interested enough in their field of expertise to ask for help. Colleges set up programs such as tutoring to help students be successful.

**Are there times when it is better to give up?** Don't give up your important goals just because you think they are difficult. However, if you realize that the goals you have set for yourself do not match your interests, it is better to set new goals and follow a different path. Prioritize how you spend your time so that you are spending it on what is most important. If you realize that the time spent on your current goal is a distraction to accomplishing more important goals, then it is better to change directions. There may be times when you must take courses that you don't consider interesting to complete your long-term goal of a college degree. In this case, it is best to think about your long-term goal of graduating from college, be gritty, and persevere.

**How can you develop grit?** The good news is that grit is related to the growth mindset and can be learned. Here are three steps for learning grit:

1. **The first step in learning grit is finding interest.** Become aware of what you enjoy doing and follow your interests. Chapter 3 in this textbook helps you to explore your interests and values.

2. **Invest your time in practice.** Find your weaknesses and strive to improve them. Practice frequently and work one small step at a time.

3. **Find your purpose.** One of the most difficult questions you may ask yourself is, "What is my purpose in life?" To answer this important question, ask yourself why your work is important and how it will help others. Knowing about your purpose helps you to maintain interest, invest your time in practice, and become passionate about your work.[9]

## Activity: How Gritty Are You?

| | Strongly Agree | Agree | Disagree | Strongly Disagree |
|---|---|---|---|---|
| I have a "never give up" attitude. | 3 | 2 | 1 | 0 |
| I spend a significant amount of time studying each week. | 3 | 2 | 1 | 0 |
| A failing grade shows a lack of intelligence. | 0 | 1 | 2 | 3 |
| Failure is an opportunity to figure out what went wrong and fix it. | 3 | 2 | 1 | 0 |
| I believe that the most talented and intelligent people will become the most successful. | 0 | 1 | 2 | 3 |
| When work is challenging, I tend to get discouraged and lose interest. | 0 | 1 | 2 | 3 |
| I have a good awareness of my interests and what I enjoy doing. | 3 | 2 | 1 | 0 |

| I can write a statement about what is my purpose in life. | 3 | 2 | 1 | 0 |
| I have goals in life and spend my time on what is most important. | 3 | 2 | 1 | 0 |
| I would describe myself as a person who has grit. | 3 | 2 | 1 | 0 |

Write your total points here: _____

| | |
|---|---|
| 25–30 | Your grittiness will help you to be successful in college, careers, and life. |
| 20–24 | You have many qualities of a gritty person, but could benefit from thinking more about how to increase your grit. |
| 15–19 | You have some qualities of a gritty person, but would benefit from re-reading the information about grit and thinking about how you can use this material to increase your success. |
| 14 or less | Re-read the material on grit and think about how you can apply it to improve your success in college. |

# Quiz

## Mindset and Grit

1.  The following is an example of the growth mindset:
    a.  Intelligence is fixed at birth.
    b.  There is a limit to what we can accomplish.
    c.  Intelligence is increased as you gain new knowledge.

2.  Research has found that the most important factor in success is
    a.  talent.
    b.  intelligence.
    c.  grit.

3.  Famous athletes, musicians, and scientist achieve success through
    a.  effortful training.
    b.  positive opportunities in life.
    c.  luck.

4.  You can develop grit by
    a.  understanding your intelligence.
    b.  doing work that is easy for you.
    c.  thinking about your purpose in life.

5.  The following statement is an example of grit:
    a.  I have a "never give up" attitude.
    b.  I believe that talented people are the most successful in life.
    c.  I think that a failing grade shows a lack of intelligence.

**How did you do on the quiz? Check your answers: 1. c, 2. c, 3. a, 4. c, 5. a**

# Journal
## Entry

Write five intention statements about using the growth mindset and grit to improve your skills.

1

# What Are Multiple Intelligences?

In 1904, the French psychologist Alfred Binet developed the IQ test, which provided a single score to measure intelligence. This once widely used and accepted test came into question because it measured the intelligence of individuals in schools in a particular culture. In different cultures and different situations, the test was less valid. As an alternative to traditional IQ tests, Harvard professor Howard Gardner developed the theory of multiple intelligences.[10] He looked at intelligence in a broader and more inclusive way than people had done in the past.

Howard Gardner observed famous musicians, artists, athletes, scientists, inventors, naturalists, and others who were recognized contributors to society to formulate a more meaningful definition of intelligence. He defined intelligence as **the human ability to solve problems or design or compose something valued in at least one culture**. His definition broadens the scope of human potential. He identified nine different intelligences: musical, interpersonal, logical-mathematical, spatial, bodily-kinesthetic, linguistic, intrapersonal, naturalist, and existential. He selected these intelligences because they are all represented by an area in the brain and are valued in different cultures. His theory can help us to understand and appreciate many different kinds of talents.

These intelligences are measured by looking at performance in activities associated with each intelligence. A key idea in this theory is that most people can develop all of their intelligences and become relatively competent in each area. Another key idea is that these intelligences work together in complex ways to make us unique. For example, an athlete uses bodily-kinesthetic intelligence to run, kick, or jump. They use spatial intelligence to keep their eye on the ball and hit it. They also need linguistic and interpersonal skills to be good members of a team.

Developing intelligences is a product of three factors:

1.  Biological endowment based on heredity and genetics
2.  Personal life history
3.  Cultural and historical background[11]

For example, Wolfgang Amadeus Mozart was born with musical talent (biological endowment). Members of his family were musicians who encouraged Mozart in music (personal life history). Mozart lived in Europe during a time when music flourished and wealthy patrons were willing to pay composers (cultural and historical background).

Each individual's life history contains **crystallizers** that promote the development of the intelligences and **paralyzers** that inhibit the development of the intelligences. These crystallizers and paralyzers often take place in early childhood. For example, Einstein was given a magnetic compass when he was four years old. He became so interested in the compass that he started on his journey of exploring the universe. An example of a paralyzer is being embarrassed or feeling humiliated about your math skills in elementary school so that you begin to lose confidence in your ability to do math. Paralyzers involve shame, guilt, fear, and anger and prevent intelligence from being developed.

This textbook includes an access code for taking the TruTalent Intelligences assessment, which assesses multiple intelligences, provides a profile of your individual strengths, and matches your results to careers with links to online career information. As you take this assessment, think positively about your skills. The following information and activities help to gain a deeper understanding of your multiple intelligences and related skills along with matching careers.

> "I have no special talent. I am only passionately curious."
> ALBERT EINSTEIN

# Journal
## Entry

Look at your results from the TruTalent Intelligences assessment. According to this assessment, what are your highest multiple intelligences? List any suggested careers in which you are interested.

**2**

# Activity

## Describing Your Multiple Intelligences

Below are some definitions and examples of the different intelligences. As you read each section, think positively about your intelligence in this area. Place a checkmark in front of each item that is true for you.

### Musical

Musical intelligence involves hearing and remembering musical patterns and manipulating patterns in music. Some occupations connected with this intelligence include musician, performer, composer, and music critic. Place a checkmark next to each skill that you possess in this area.

_____ I enjoy singing, humming, or whistling.

_____ One of my interests is playing recorded music.

_____ I have collections of recorded music.

_____ I play or used to play a musical instrument.

_____ I can play the drums or tap out rhythms.

_____ I appreciate music.

_____ Music affects how I feel.

_____ I enjoy having music on while working or studying.

_____ I can clap my hands and keep time to music.

_____ I can tell when a musical note is off key.

_____ I remember melodies and the words to songs.

_____ I have participated in a band, chorus, or other musical group.

Look at the items you have checked above and summarize your musical intelligence.

_____

_____

_____

## Interpersonal

Interpersonal intelligence is defined as understanding people. Occupations connected with this intelligence involve working with people and helping them, as in education or health care. Place a checkmark next to each skill that you possess in this area.

_____ I enjoy being around people.

_____ I am sensitive to other people's feelings.

_____ I am a good listener.

_____ I understand how others feel.

_____ I have many friends.

_____ I enjoy parties and social gatherings.

_____ I enjoy participating in groups.

_____ I can get people to cooperate and work together.

_____ I am involved in clubs or community activities.

_____ People come to me for advice.

_____ I am a peacemaker.

_____ I enjoy helping others.

Look at the items you have checked above and summarize your interpersonal intelligence.

_____

_____

_____

## Logical-Mathematical

Logical-mathematical intelligence involves understanding abstract principles and manipulating numbers, quantities, and operations. Some examples of occupations associated with logical-mathematical intelligence are mathematician, tax accountant, scientist, and computer programmer. Place a checkmark next to each skill that you possess. Keep an open mind. People usually either love or hate this area.

_____   I can do arithmetic problems quickly.

_____   I enjoy math.

_____   I enjoy doing puzzles.

_____   I enjoy working with computers.

_____   I am interested in computer programming.

_____   I enjoy science classes.

_____   I enjoy doing the experiments in lab science courses.

_____   I can look at information and outline it easily.

_____   I understand charts and diagrams.

_____   I enjoy playing chess or checkers.

_____   I use logic to solve problems.

_____   I can organize things and keep them in order.

Look at the items you have checked above and summarize your logical-mathematical intelligence.

_____

_____

_____

## Spatial

Spatial intelligence involves the ability to manipulate objects in space. For example, a baseball player uses spatial intelligence to hit a ball. Occupations associated with spatial intelligence include pilot, painter, sculptor, architect, inventor, and surgeon. This intelligence is often used in athletics, the arts, or the sciences. Place a checkmark next to each skill that you possess in this area.

_____   I can appreciate a good photograph or piece of art.

_____   I think in pictures and images.

_____   I can use visualization to remember.

_____   I can easily read maps, charts, and diagrams.

_____   I participate in artistic activities (art, drawing, painting, photography).

_____   I know which way is north, south, east, and west.

_____   I can put things together.

_____   I enjoy jigsaw puzzles or mazes.

_____    I enjoy seeing movies, slides, or photographs.

_____    I can appreciate good design.

_____    I enjoy using telescopes, microscopes, or binoculars.

_____    I understand color, line, shape, and form.

Look at the items you have checked above and summarize your spatial intelligence.

_____

_____

_____

## Bodily-Kinesthetic

Bodily-kinesthetic intelligence is defined as being able to use your body to solve problems. People with bodily-kinesthetic intelligence make or invent objects or perform. They learn by doing, touching, and handling. Occupations connected to this type of intelligence include athlete, performer (dancer, actor), craftsperson, sculptor, mechanic, and surgeon. Place a checkmark next to each skill that you possess in this area.

_____    I am good at using my hands.

_____    I have good coordination and balance.

_____    I learn best by moving around and touching things.

_____    I participate in physical activities or sports.

_____    I learn new sports easily.

_____    I enjoy watching sports events.

_____    I am skilled in a craft such as woodworking, sewing, art, or fixing machines.

_____    I have good manual dexterity.

_____    I find it difficult to sit still for a long time.

_____    I prefer to be up and moving.

_____    I am good at dancing and remember dance steps easily.

_____    It was easy for me to learn to ride a bike or skateboard.

Look at the items you checked above and describe your bodily-kinesthetic intelligence.

_____

_____

_____

## Linguistic

People with linguistic intelligence are good with language and words. They have good reading, writing, and speaking skills. Linguistic intelligence is an asset in any occupation. Specific related careers include writing, education, and politics. Place a checkmark next to each skill that you possess in this area.

_____ I am a good writer.

_____ I am a good reader.

_____ I enjoy word games and crossword puzzles.

_____ I can tell jokes and stories.

_____ I am good at explaining.

_____ I can remember names, places, facts, and trivia.

_____ I'm generally good at spelling.

_____ I have a good vocabulary.

_____ I read for fun and relaxation.

_____ I am good at memorizing.

_____ I enjoy group discussions.

_____ I have a journal or diary.

Look at the items you have checked above and summarize your linguistic intelligence.

_____

_____

_____

## Intrapersonal

Intrapersonal intelligence is the ability to understand yourself and how to best use your natural talents and abilities. Examples of careers associated with this intelligence include novelist, psychologist, or being self-employed. Place a checkmark next to each skill that you possess in this area.

_____ I understand and accept my strengths and weaknesses.

_____ I am very independent.

_____ I am self-motivated.

_____ I have definite opinions on controversial issues.

_____ I enjoy quiet time alone to pursue a hobby or work on a project.

_____ I am self-confident.

_____ I can work independently.

_____ I can help others with self-understanding.

_____ I appreciate quiet time for concentration.

_____ I am aware of my own feelings and sensitive to others.

_____ I am self-directed.

_____ I enjoy reflecting on ideas and concepts.

Look at the items you have checked above and summarize your intrapersonal intelligence.

_____

_____

_____

## Naturalist

The naturalist is able to recognize, classify, and analyze plants, animals, and cultural artifacts. Occupations associated with this intelligence include botanist, horticulturist, biologist, archeologist, and environmental occupations. Place a checkmark next to each skill you possess in this area.

_____ I know the names of minerals, plants, trees, and animals.

_____ I think it is important to preserve our natural environment.

_____ I enjoy taking classes in the natural sciences such as biology.

_____ I enjoy the outdoors.

_____ I take care of flowers, plants, trees, or animals.

_____ I am interested in archeology or geology.

_____ I would enjoy a career involved in protecting the environment.

_____ I have or used to have a collection of rocks, shells, or insects.

_____ I belong to organizations interested in protecting the environment.

_____ I think it is important to protect endangered species.

_____ I enjoy camping or hiking.

_____ I appreciate natural beauty.

Look at the items you have checked above and describe your naturalist intelligence.

_____

_____

_____

### Existential

Existential intelligence is the capacity to ask profound questions about the meaning of life and death. This intelligence is the cornerstone of art, religion, and philosophy. Related occupations include minister, philosopher, psychologist, and artist. Place a checkmark next to each skill that you possess in this area.

_____    I often think about the meaning and purpose of life.

_____    I have strong personal beliefs and convictions.

_____    I enjoy thinking about abstract theories.

_____    I have considered being a philosopher, scientist, theologian, or artist.

_____    I often read books that are philosophical or imaginative.

_____    I enjoy reading science fiction.

_____    I like to work independently.

_____    I like to search for meaning in my studies.

_____    I wonder if there are other intelligent life forms in the universe.

Look at the items you have checked above and describe your existential intelligence.

_____

_____

_____

## Journal Entry

Look at the above charts and see where you have the most checkmarks. What do you think are your highest intelligences? Do your opinions match the results on the TruTalent multiple intelligences assessment?

**3**

## Build on Your Strengths

Consider your personal strengths when deciding on a career. People in each of the multiple intelligence areas have different strengths:

- Musical strengths include listening to music, singing, playing a musical instrument, keeping a beat, and recognizing musical patterns. People with this intelligence are "musical smart."
- Interpersonal strengths include communication skills, social skills, helping others, understanding others' feelings, and the ability to resolve conflicts. People with this intelligence are "people smart."

- Logical-mathematical strengths include math aptitude, interest in science, problem solving skills, and logical thinking. People with this intelligence are "number/reasoning smart."
- Spatial strengths include visualization, understanding puzzles, navigation, visual arts, reading, and writing. People with this intelligence are "picture smart."
- Bodily-kinesthetic strengths include hand and eye coordination, athletics, dance, drama, cooking, sculpting, and learning by doing. People with this intelligence are "body smart."
- Linguistic strengths include good reading, writing, vocabulary, and spelling skills; good communication skills; being a good listener; having a good memory, and learning new languages easily. People with this intelligence are "word smart."
- Intrapersonal strengths include good self-awareness. They are aware of their feelings and emotions and are often independent and self-motivated to achieve. People with this intelligence are "self-smart."
- Naturalist strengths include exploring and preserving the environment and are very aware of natural surroundings. People with this intelligence are "nature smart."
- Existential strengths include reflecting on important questions about the universe, the purpose of life, and religious beliefs. People with this intelligence are "curiosity smart."

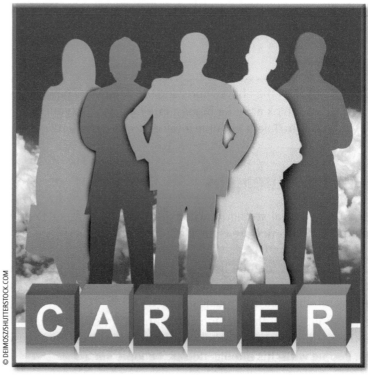

© DEIMOSZ/SHUTTERSTOCK.COM

# Activity

In what areas are you "smart?"

_____

_____

_____

_____

_____

## Some Careers and Multiple Intelligences

Circle any careers that seem interesting to you.

| Musical | Interpersonal | Logical-Mathematical |
|---|---|---|
| Disc Jockey | Cruise Director | Engineer |
| Music Teacher | Mediator | Accountant |
| Music Retailer | Human Resources | Computer Analyst |
| Music Therapist | Dental Hygienist | Physician |
| Recording Engineer | Nurse | Detective |
| Singer | Psychologist | Researcher |
| Song Writer | Social Worker | Scientist |
| Speech Pathologist | Administrator | Computer Programmer |
| Music Librarian | Marketer | Database Designer |
| Choir Director | Religious Leader | Physicist |
| Music Critic | Teacher | Auditor |
| Music Lawyer | Counselor | Economist |

| Spatial | Bodily-Kinesthetic | Linguistic |
|---|---|---|
| Architect | Athlete | Journalist |
| Artist | Carpenter | Writer |
| Film Animator | Craftsperson | Editor |
| Mechanic | Mechanic | Attorney |
| Pilot | Jeweler | Curator |
| Webmaster | Computer Game Designer | Newscaster |
| Interior Decorator | Firefighter | Politician |
| Graphic Artist | Forest Ranger | Speech Pathologist |
| Sculptor | Physical Therapist | Translator |
| Surveyor | Personal Trainer | Comedian |
| Urban Planner | Surgeon | Historian |
| Photographer | Recreation Specialist | Librarian |
|  |  | Marketing Consultant |

"The best years of your life are the ones in which you decide your problems are your own. You do not blame them on your mother, the ecology, or the president. You realize that you control your own destiny."

ALBERT ELLIS

| Intrapersonal | Naturalist | Existential |
|---|---|---|
| Career Counselor | Park Ranger | Counselor |
| Wellness Counselor | Dog Trainer | Psychologist |
| Therapist | Landscaper | Psychiatrist |
| Criminologist | Meteorologist | Social Worker |
| intelligence Officer | Veterinarian | Ministry |
| Entrepreneur | Animal Health Technician | Philosopher |
| Psychologist | Ecologist | Artist |
| Researcher | Nature Photographer | Scientist |
| Actor | Wilderness Guide | Researcher |
| Artist | Anthropologist | Motivational Speaker |
| Philosopher | Environmental Lawyer | Human Resources |
| Writer | Water Conservationist | Writer |

# Using Emotional Intelligence

Emotional intelligence is related to interpersonal and intrapersonal intelligences. It is the ability to recognize, control, and evaluate your own emotions while realizing how they affect people around you. Emotional intelligence affects career success, because it is related to our ability to express ourselves, work as part of a team, concentrate, remember, make decisions, deal with stress, overcome challenges, deal with conflict, and empathize with others. Research has shown emotional intelligence can predict career success and that workers with high emotional intelligence are more likely to end up in leadership positions in which they are happy with their jobs.[12]

The premise of emotional intelligence is that you can be more successful if you are aware of your own emotions as well as the emotions of others. There are two aspects of emotional intelligence:

- Understanding yourself, your goals, intentions, responses, and behavior.
- Understanding others and their feelings.

Daniel Goleman has identified the five most important characteristics of emotional intelligence:[13]

1. **Self-Awareness.** People with high emotional intelligence are aware of their emotions, including strengths and weaknesses.

2. **Self-Regulation.** This involves the ability to control emotions and impulses. Being impulsive can lead to careless decisions like attending a party the night before a final exam. Characteristics of self-regulation include comfort with change, integrity, and the ability to say no.

3. **Motivation.** People with high emotional intelligence can defer immediate results for long-term success. For example, investing your time in education can lead to future career opportunities and income.

4. **Empathy.** Empathy is the ability to understand the needs and viewpoints of others around you and avoiding stereotypes. It involves good listening skills that enhance personal relationships.

5. **Social Skills.** People with good social skills are good team players and willing to help others to be successful.

You can enhance your career success by developing your emotional intelligence. Here are some tips for improving your emotional intelligence and managing personal relationships on the job.

- Be empathetic when working with others by trying to put yourself in their place to understand different perspectives and points of view. Don't be quick to jump to conclusions or stereotype others.
- Think about how your actions affect others. Always treat others as you would like to be treated.
- Be open-minded and intellectually curious. Consider the opinions of others in a positive manner. Be willing to examine and change your mindset.
- Give others credit for their accomplishments in the workplace. When speaking about your own accomplishments, confidently state what you did without trying to seek too much attention.
- Evaluate your own strengths and weaknesses. Focus on your strengths, but be aware of the weaknesses and work to improve them. The personality assessment in Chapter 2 helps you to understand your personal strengths and weaknesses.
- Work on stress management by finding some stress reduction techniques that work for you. In stressful situations, it is helpful to remain calm and in control. Seek workable solutions without blaming others. Your college health services office often provides workshops on stress management.
- Take a college course to improve verbal as well as nonverbal communication. When talking with others, focus on what they are saying rather than what you are going to say next. Learn how to make "I statements" that effectively communicate your thoughts without blaming others. Become aware of nonverbal communication, which adds a significant dimension to communication.
- Use humor to help you deal with challenges. Humor helps you to keep things in perspective, deal with differences, relax, and come up with creative solutions.
- Deal with conflicts in a way that builds trust. Focus on win-win solutions that allow both parties to have their needs met.
- Take responsibility for your actions. Admit when you make mistakes and work to improve the situation in the future.
- Use critical thinking to analyze the pros and cons of the situation.
- Be goal oriented and focus on the task and the steps needed to achieve your goals.
- Be optimistic. Optimism leads to greater opportunities and results in better personal relationships.

© ARKA38/SHUTTERSTOCK.COM

# Quiz

## Multiple Intelligences

Test what you have learned by selecting the correct answers to the following questions.

**1.** Multiple intelligences are defined as
   **a.** the many parts of intelligence as measured by an IQ test.
   **b.** the ability to design something valued in at least one culture.
   **c.** the ability to read, write, and do mathematical computations.

**2.** The concept of multiple intelligences is significant because
   **a.** it measures the intelligence of students in schools.
   **b.** it does not use culture in measuring intelligence.
   **c.** it broadens the scope of human potential and includes all cultures.

**3.** Intelligences are measured by
   **a.** IQ tests.
   **b.** performance in activities related to the intelligence.
   **c.** performance in the classroom.

**4.** Each individual's life history contains crystallizers that
   **a.** promote the development of the intelligences.
   **b.** inhibit the development of the intelligences.
   **c.** cause the individual to be set in their ways.

**5.** Emotional intelligence involves
   **a.** self-criticism.
   **b.** self-awareness.
   **c.** self-doubt.

**How did you do on the quiz? Check your answers: 1. b, 2. c, 3. b, 4. a, 5. b**

## Journal Entry

Comment on your emotional intelligence and how you can use it to be successful in your career.

**4**

# Keys to Success
## Persistence and Grit

There is an old saying that persistence will get you almost anything eventually. Current research on college success supports this idea. The key idea is that aptitude does not guarantee success. Persistence and grit are more important. If you are persistent and gritty, you have the motivation to use effortful practice to improve any skills that are important for your future career.

It has been said that 99% of success is just showing up. Any faculty member will tell you that the number one reason for students dropping out of college is lack of attendance. They know that when students miss three classes in a row, they are not likely to return. Even very cabable students who miss class may find that they are lost when they come back.  Many students are simply afraid to return. Classes such as math and foreign languages are sequential, and it is very difficult to make up work after an absence. One of the most important ways you can be successful is to make a habit of consistently showing up for class.

Although attendance is the crucial first step, it is not enough. You will also need commitment to be successful. Commitment is a promise to yourself to follow through with something. In athletics, it is not necessarily the one with the best physical skills who makes the best athlete. Commitment and practice make a great athlete. Commitment means doing whatever is necessary to succeed. Like the good athlete, make a commitment to accomplishing your goals. Spend the time necessary to be successful in your studies.

When you face difficulties, persistence and commitment are especially important. History is full of famous people who contributed to society through persistence and commitment. Consider the following facts about Abraham Lincoln, for example.

- Failed in business at age 21.
- Was defeated in a legislative race at age 22.
- Failed again in business at age 24.
- Overcame the death of his sweetheart at age 26.
- Had a nervous breakdown at age 27.
- Lost a congressional race at age 34.
- Lost a congressional race at age 36.
- Lost a senatorial race at age 45.
- Failed in an effort to become vice president at age 47.
- Lost a senatorial race at age 49.
- Was elected president of the United States at age 52.[10]

© GUSTAVO FRAZAO/SHUTTERSTOCK.COM

The goal of getting a college education and finding your dream job may seem like a mountain that is difficult to climb. Break it into smaller steps that you can accomplish. See your college counselor or advisor, register for classes, attend the first class, read the first chapter, do the first assignment, work on your career plan, and you will be on the road to success. Then continue to break tasks into small, achievable steps and continue from one step to the next. And remember, persistence will get you almost anything eventually.

## Journal Entry

What will you do if you are tempted to drop out of college? What steps can you take to be persistent in achieving your college goals? Are there times when it is best to change goals rather than to be persistent if your efforts are not working? Write a paragraph about how you will be persistent in reaching your college and career goals.

## JOURNAL ENTRIES
## EXPLORING YOUR MULTIPLE INTELLIGENCES

Go to http://www.collegesuccess1.com/JournalEntries.htm for Word files of the Journal Entries.

## SUCCESS over the Internet

Visit the *College Success Website* at http://www.collegesuccess1.com/

The *College Success Website* is continually updated with new topics and links to the material presented in this chapter. Topics include:

- Mindset
- Grit
- Multiple intelligences
- Emotional intelligence
- Goal setting

Contact your instructor if you have any problems in accessing the *College Success Website.*

# Notes

1. Carol Dweck, *Mindset, The New Psychology of Success* (New York: Ballantine Books, 2016).
2. Angela Duckworth, *Grit: The Power of Passion and Perseverance,* (New York: Simon & Schuster, 2016).
3. Ibid., 14.
4. Ibid., 29.
5. Retrieved from https://www.quora.com/How-many-hours-a-week-does-an-NBA-player-work-during-the-season, July 2017.
6. Retrieved from http://patriotswire.usatoday.com/2017/02/02/behind-tom-bradys-preparation-for-super-bowl-li/, July 2017.
7. Aimee Simeon, "The Next Time You're Feeling Lazy, Remember That Simon Biles Trains 32 Hours Every Week," March 12, 2016, https://www.popsugar.com/fitness/Simone-Biles-Ellen-DeGeneres-Show-March-2016-40475107
8. Retrieved from http://www.thestrad.com/violinist-itzhak-perlman-talks-about-practice/, July 2017.
9. Duckworth, p. 91.
10. Howard Gardner, *Intelligence Reframed: Multiple Intelligences for the Twenty-First Century* (Boulder, CO: Basic Books, 1999).
11. Thomas Armstrong, *Multiple Intelligences in the Classroom* (Alexandria, VA: Association for Curriculum Development, 1994).
12. "Emotional Intelligence in Career Planning," accessed August 2013, https://www1.cfnc.org/
13. "Emotional Intelligence, Developing Strong People Skills," accessed August 2013, http://www.mindtools.com/pages/article/newCDV_59.htm
14. Viktor Frankl, *Man's Search for Meaning* (New York: Pocket Books, 1963), 104–105.
15. Quoted in Rob Gilbert, ed., *Bits and Pieces,* November 4, 1999.
16. Stephen Covey, *The 7 Habits of Highly Effective People* (New York: Simon and Schuster, 1989), 71.
17. Ibid., 75.
18. Anthony Robbins, Unlimited Power (New York: Ballantine Books, 1986), 73.

# MULTIPLE INTELLIGENCES MATCHING QUIZ

Directions: Match the person with the intelligence at the right:

____Michael Jordan

____Aristotle

____Martin Luther King, Jr.

____Sigmund Freud

____William Shakespeare

____Albert Einstein

____William James "will.i.am"

____Charles Darwin

____George Lucas

A    Musical: hearing and remembering musical patterns

B    Interpersonal: understanding other people

C    Mathematical: working with numbers

D    Spatial: manipulating objects in space

E    Bodily–Kinesthetic: using your body

F    Linguistic: using language

G    Intrapersonal: understanding yourself

H    Naturalist: understanding the environment

I    Existential: pondering the meaning of life and our place in the universe

Work with other students in a group to give examples of other famous person's in these categories.

Musical

Interpersonal

Mathematical

Spatial

Bodily–Kinesthetic

Linguistic

Intrapersonal

Naturalist

Existential

# CRYSTALLIZERS AND PARALYZERS

Complete the "Describing Your Multiple Intelligences" activity in this chapter before doing this exercise.

Each individual's life history contains **crystallizers** that promote the development of intelligences. Look at your highest scores on the multiple intelligences activity. List your highest scores below. Write down at least two crystallizers you experienced that may have helped you to develop these intelligences. For example, you may have been praised for your athletic skills and developed your bodily-kinesthetic intelligence.

My highest scores:

Crystallizers:

Each individual's life history also contains paralyzers that inhibit the development of intelligences. Look at your lowest scores on the multiple intelligences activity. Write down two paralyzers that may have discouraged you from developing this intelligence. For example, maybe you had a bad experience with math in elementary or middle school. Paralyzers often involve shame, guilt, fear, or anger.

My lowest scores:

Paralyzers:

# Planning Your Career and Education

# 5

## Learning
## OBJECTIVES

Read to answer these key questions:

- What are some employment trends for the future?

- What are work skills necessary for success in the twenty-first century?

- How do I research a career?

- How do I plan my education?

- How can I make good decisions about my future?

- What is a dangerous opportunity?

It is always easier to get where you are going if you have a road map or a plan. To start the journey, it is helpful to know about yourself, including your personality, interests, talents, and values. Once you have this picture, you will need to know about the world of work and job trends that will affect your future employment opportunities. Next, you will need to make decisions about which road to follow. Then, you will need to plan your education to reach your destination. Finally, you will need some job-seeking skills such a writing a resume and cover letter, using social media to market yourself online, and preparing for a successful interview.

© KISELEV ANDREY VALEREVICH/SHUTTERSTOCK.COM

## Keep Your Eyes on the Future

"What is the recipe for successful achievement? To my mind there are just four essential ingredients: Choose a career you love, give it the best there is in you, seize your opportunities, and be a member of the team."

BENJAMIN FAIRLESS

The world is changing quickly, and these changes will affect your future career. To assure your future career success, you will need to become aware of career trends and observe how they change over time so that you can adjust your career plans accordingly. For example, recently a school was established for training bank tellers. The school quickly went out of business and the students demanded their money back because they were not able to get jobs. A careful observer of career trends would have noticed that bank tellers are being replaced by automatic teller machines (ATMs) and would not have started a school for training bank tellers. Students observant of career trends would not have paid money for the training. It is probably a good idea for bank tellers to look ahead and plan a new career direction.

How can you find out about career trends that may affect you in the future? Become a careful observer by reading about current events. Good sources of information include:

• Your local newspaper, especially the business section
• News programs
• Current magazines
• Government statistics and publications
• The Internet

When thinking about future trends, use your critical thinking skills. Sometimes trends change quickly or interact in different ways. For example, since we are using email to a great extent today, it might seem that mail carriers would not be as much in demand in the future. However, since people are buying more goods over the Internet, there has been an increased demand for mail carriers and other delivery services. Develop the habit of looking at what is happening to see if you can identify trends that may affect your future.

Usually trends get started as a way to meet the following needs:[1]

- To save money
- To reduce cost
- To do things faster
- To make things easier to use
- To improve safety and reliability
- To lessen the impact on the environment

The following are some trends to watch that may affect your future career. As you read about each trend, think about how it could affect you.

## Baby Boomers, Generation X, Millennials, Generation Z, and the New Generation Alpha

About every 20 years, sociologists begin to describe a new generation with similar characteristics based on shared historical experiences. Each generation has different opportunities and challenges in the workplace.

**The Baby Boomers were born following World War II between 1946 and 1964.** Four out of every 10 adults today are in this Baby Boom Generation.[2] Think about the implications of an older population. Older people need such things as health care, recreation, travel, and financial planning. Occupations related to these needs are likely to be in demand now and in the future.

**Those born between 1965 and 1977 are often referred to as Generation X.** They are sometimes called the "baby bust" generation because fewer babies were born during this period than in the previous generations. There is much in the media about this generation having to pay higher taxes and Social Security payments to support the large number of aging Baby Boomers. Some say that this generation will not enjoy the prosperity of the Baby Boomers. Those who left college in the early nineties faced a recession and the worst job market since World War II.[3] Many left college in debt and returned home to live with their parents. Because of a lack of employment opportunities, many in this generation became entrepreneurs, starting new companies at a faster rate than previous generations.

Jane Bryant Quinn notes that in spite of economic challenges, Generation Xers have a lot going for them:[4]

- They have record-high levels of education, which correlate with higher income and lower unemployment.

- Generation Xers are computer literate, and those who use computers on the job earn 10 to 15 percent more than those who don't.
- This group often has a good work ethic valued by employers. However, they value a balanced lifestyle with time for outside interests and family.
- As Baby Boomers retire, more job opportunities are created for this group.
- Unlike the Baby Boomers, this generation was born into a more integrated and more diverse society. They are better able than previous generations to adapt to diversity in society and the workplace.

**Those in the New Millennial Generation were born between 1977 and 1995.** This generation is sometimes called Generation Y or the Echo Boomers, since they are the children of the Baby Boomers.[5] This new generation of approximately 60 million is three times larger than Generation X and will eventually exceed the number of Baby Boomers.

Millennials are more ethnically diverse than previous generations with 34 percent ethnic minorities. One in four lives with a single parent; three in four have working mothers. Most of them started using computers before they were five years old. Marketing researchers describe this new generation as "technologically adept, info-savvy, a cyber-generation, the clickeratti."[6] They are the connected generation, accustomed to cell phones, chatting on the Internet, and listening to downloaded music.

Young people in the Millennial Generation share a different historical perspective from the Baby Boom Generation. Baby Boomers remember the Vietnam War and the assassinations of President John F. Kennedy and Martin Luther King. For Millennials, school shootings such as Columbine and Parkland will forever be in their memories along with acts of terrorism such as the Oklahoma City bombing and the 9–11 attack on New York City. The Millennial Generation will see their main problems as dealing with violence, easy access to weapons, the threat of terrorism, and social justice issues.

Neil Howe and William Strauss paint a very positive picture of this new generation in their book *Millennials Rising: The Next Great Generation*:

- Millennials will rebel by tearing down old institutions that do not work and building new and better institutions. The authors predict that this will be the can-do generation filled with technology planners, community shapers, institution builders, and world leaders.
- Surveys show that this generation describes themselves as happy, confident, and positive.
- They are cooperative team players.
- They generally accept authority and respect their parents' values.
- They follow rules. The rates of homicides, violent crime, abortion, and teen pregnancy are decreasing rapidly.
- The use of alcohol, drugs, and tobacco is decreasing.
- Millennials have a fascination with and mastery of new technology.
- Their most important values are individuality and uniqueness.[7]

In the past, new generations emerged about every twenty years. However, because of rapid social change, generations are now being defined in shorter time periods. **Those in Generation Z were born between 1995 and 2010.** Various names for this generation include Generation Z, Generation Wii, the iGeneration, Gen Tech, Digital Natives, Net Gen, and the Plurals.[8] These names reflect this generation's fascination and ease of using technology as well as their increasing diversity. This is a large generation with one in four Americans under 18 years old.[9]

This generation has been affected by historical events such as the election of President Obama (the first biracial president), events surrounding 9/11, wars in Iraq and Afghanistan, the tsunami and nuclear meltdown in Japan, school violence, and economic recession. This is the generation most impacted by the Pandemic of 2020-21 which occurred as this generation completed their education and moved into the workforce. They are referred to as digital natives since they have always lived in a world with the Internet, smart phones, and other devices.

Some characteristic of this new generation include:[10]

- This is the last generation with a Caucasian majority. Only 55% of this generation is Caucasian as compared to 72% of Baby Boomers. In 2019, less than 50% of births will be Caucasian.

- They are more positive than older Americans about becoming an ethnically diverse society and more likely to have friends from different racial, ethnic, and religious groups.

- There is a continuing decline in two-parent households with only two out of three people from two parent households. Increased same sex marriage is changing the definition of family.

- Women are more likely to get a college degree and hold 51% of managerial and professional jobs. As a result, gender roles are blending with men assuming more familial responsibilities.

- It is an age of "girl power." Girls ages 8–15 care more about their grades than boys and have more expectations of receiving a college degree and having work that changes the world.
- Technology will continue to influence this group as in the New Millennial Generation. Use of technology will transform the way that people communicate and purchase goods. People will communicate with shorter and more immediate communications such as texting and Twitter. More purchases will be made on the Internet.
- This generation hopes to use technology as a tool to change the world.

It is predicted that the world of work for both the Millennials and Generation Z will be dramatically different. Previous generations anticipated having a lifetime career. By the year 2020, many jobs will probably be short-term contracts. This arrangement will provide cost savings and efficiency for employers and flexibility for employees to start or stop work to take vacations, train for new jobs, or meet family responsibilities. One in five people will be self-employed. Retirement will be postponed as people look forward to living longer and healthier lives.[11]

**Generation Alpha is the current generation of children born since 2010.** This new generation is called Generation Alpha because they are the start of something new, born entirely in the twenty-first century.[12] They will remember their parents working from home or being unemployed while they experienced virtual learning from home during the pandemic of 2020–21. Technology is becoming an even more important part of their lives, and they will find more creative uses for it in the future.

This generation is facing great uncertainty, rapid changes in society, and changing economic opportunities that will impact their personal and professional lives. This generation will face these new emerging trends:

- Health and economic challenges resulting from the COVID-19 pandemic of 2020–21
- Increasing threats from climate change
- Lack of access to healthcare
- The effects of racial injustice
- Decrease in civility and increased divisions in society
- Need for mental health services because of increased anxiety and stress

Impacts from these events will be determined by how society deals with these issues in the next few years. One positive result could be greater resilience as this generation watches people coming together to help others in times of need.

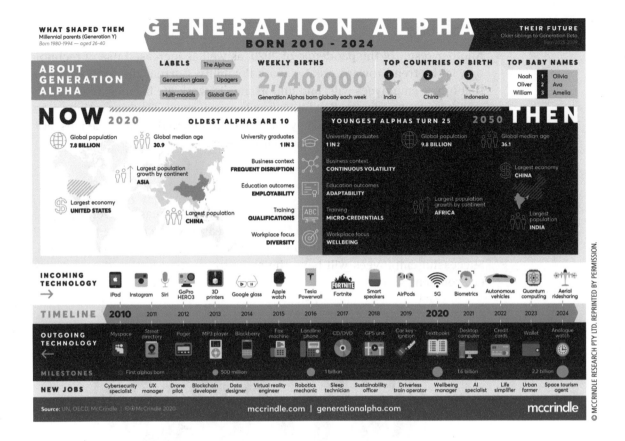

## Journal Entry

Describe your generation (Baby Boomer, Generation X, New Millennial, Generation Z, or Generation Alpha). What are your best qualities and challenges?

**1**

# Career Trends 2019–2029

The following are some trends to watch that may affect your future career. As you read about each trend, think about how it could affect your future. For specific information about career trends and your major, search the US Bureau of Labor Statistics site at https://www.bls.gov/.

## Working from Home

As a result of the pandemic of 2020, more people are working at home. Currently, approximately 58 percent of the workforce is working from home. A hybrid model of working from home and attending office meetings will allow for greater productivity, collaboration, and socialization.

## Flexibility

Another result of the pandemic of 2020, as well as increased use of technology, is the trend toward greater work flexibility. Current research suggests that future employees will "find importance in work/life balance, team focus, empowerment, support, flexibility, involvement, creativity, innovation and a global working atmosphere. They are also characterized by multiple jobs, lifelong learning, multiple careers and entrepreneurship".[13]

## Diversity at Work

Most employers (78 percent) believe in the value of increased diversity in the workplace. Productivity and profits are increased when diverse people feel appreciated and can work collaboratively to come up with creative solutions. Successful employees will have the skills to function in this diverse work environment.[14]

© RAWPIXEL.COM/SHUTTERSTOCK.COM

## Preference for Soft Skills

Soft skills include empathy, emotional intelligence, creativity, and communication skills. In a survey by LinkedIn, 92 percent of human resources managers considered soft skills more important than other skills required for the job.[15]

© TRUEFFELPIX/SHUTTERSTOCK.COM

## Green Jobs

Green jobs are occupations dealing with the efficient use of energy, finding renewable sources of energy, and preserving the environment. Jobs in this field include engineers who design new technology, consultants who audit energy needs, and technicians who install and maintain systems. Here are some green job titles: environmental lawyer, environmental engineer, sustainability consultant, green architect, green building project manager, marine biologist, environmental technician, energy efficiency specialist, organic farmer, compliance manager, product engineer, wind energy engineer, solar engineer, and solar installer.

© ZHANG KAN/SHUTTERSTOCK.COM

## Finance and Business

Money management has become increasingly complex and important requiring professionals who understand finance, investments, and taxes. Today's business managers need to understand increased competition, the global economy, and must stay up to date with the latest forms of communication and social media. Businesses will increasingly rely on virtual collaboration. The median salaries in this category range from $70,000 to $80,000 and beyond, making this occupation a good choice for those interested in higher incomes. Jobs with fast growth include market research analysts, marketing specialists, personal financial advisors, and health care managers.

## Entrepreneurship and Small Business

Small businesses that can find innovative ways of meeting customer needs will be in demand for the future. A growing number of entrepreneurs operate their small businesses from home, taking advantage of telecommunication and the Internet to communicate with customers. While there is increased risk involved, the benefits include flexible scheduling, being your own boss, taking charge of your destiny, and greater potential income.

## Higher Earnings in STEM Occupations

The median annual wage for science, technology, engineering, and math (STEM) occupations in 2019 was $86,980 as compared to $38,160 for non-STEM occupations. The job outlook in this area remains high. Develop your skills in these areas to improve your employment prospects.[16]

"One child, one teacher, one book, one pen can change the world."
MALALA YOUSAFZAI

## Increased Need for Education

Constant change in society and innovation in technology will require lifelong learning on the job. Education will take place in a variety of forms: community college courses, training on the job, online learning, and learning on your own. Those who do not keep up with new technology will quickly find their job skills becoming obsolete. Higher education is linked to greater earnings and increased employment opportunities.

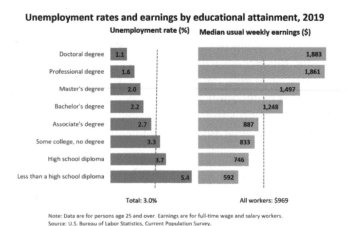

Note: Data are for persons age 25 and over. Earnings are for full-time wage and salary workers.
Source: U.S. Bureau of Labor Statistics, Current Population Survey.

Source: US Bureau of Labor Statistics, "Unemployment Rates and Earnings by Educational Attainment," last modified September 4, 2019, https://www.bls.gov/emp/chart-unemployment-earnings-education.htm.

## Increasing Opportunities in Healthcare, Social Service, Computer, and Mathematical Occupations

Careers include mental health workers, nurse practitioners, occupational therapy assistants, physician assistants, computer security, software developers, and information security.

## 6 of the 10 Fastest Growing Occupations are Related to Healthcare

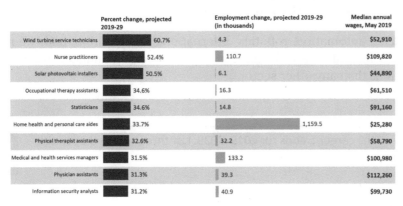

| | Percent change, projected 2019-29 | Employment change, projected 2019-29 (in thousands) | Median annual wages, May 2019 |
|---|---|---|---|
| Wind turbine service technicians | 60.7% | 4.3 | $52,910 |
| Nurse practitioners | 52.4% | 110.7 | $109,820 |
| Solar photovoltaic installers | 50.5% | 6.1 | $44,890 |
| Occupational therapy assistants | 34.6% | 16.3 | $61,510 |
| Statisticians | 34.6% | 14.8 | $91,160 |
| Home health and personal care aides | 33.7% | 1,159.5 | $25,280 |
| Physical therapist assistants | 32.6% | 32.2 | $58,790 |
| Medical and health services managers | 31.5% | 133.2 | $100,980 |
| Physician assistants | 31.3% | 39.3 | $112,260 |
| Information security analysts | 31.2% | 40.9 | $99,730 |

Source: US Bureau of Labor Statistics, "6 of the 10 Fastest Growing Occupations Are Related to Healthcare," https://www.bls.gov/emp/images/growing_occupations.png.

## Projected Percent Change, by Selected Occupational Groups, 2019-29

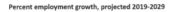

Percent employment growth, projected 2019-2029

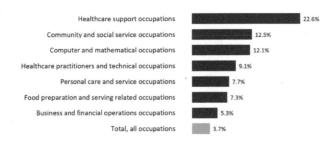

| | |
|---|---|
| Healthcare support occupations | 22.6% |
| Community and social service occupations | 12.5% |
| Computer and mathematical occupations | 12.1% |
| Healthcare practitioners and technical occupations | 9.1% |
| Personal care and service occupations | 7.7% |
| Food preparation and serving related occupations | 7.3% |
| Business and financial operations occupations | 5.3% |
| Total, all occupations | 3.7% |

Source: US Bureau of Labor Statistics, "Projected Percent Change by Selected Occupational Groups, 2019–29," https://www.bls.gov/emp/images/percent_change.png.

# Technological Advancement

Advances in technology will lead to increased employment in professional, business, and scientific services. Careers include computer systems design and consulting services related to management, scientific, and technical consulting. New developments in artificial intelligence will increasingly be used in robots and smart machines.[17]

# Declining Careers in Manufacturing, Retail Trade, Sales, and Administrative Support

Increased automation, robotics, international competition, and the rise in e-commerce will cause declines in these careers. Manufacturing will lose more jobs than any other sector.[18]

## Journal Entry    2

Do a quick review of the career trends for 2019–2029. List three trends that could affect your future.

1.

2.

3.

Go to the US Bureau of Labor Statistics site at https://www.bls.gov/ and search for any career you may be considering. Briefly list two interesting or helpful ideas you found at this site.

4.

5.

## Quiz

### Career Trends of the Future

Test what you have learned by selecting the correct answers to the following questions:

1.  A new trend for the future is
    a.  more structure on the job.
    b.  greater flexibility and working from home.
    c.  decreased diversity in the workplace.

2.  Soft skills include
    a.  skills specific to the job.
    b.  basic skills such as reading, math, and communication.
    c.  empathy, emotional intelligence, creativity, and good communication skills.

3.  Six out of ten of the fastest-growing occupations are related to
    a.  healthcare.
    b.  manufacturing.
    c.  retail trade, sales, and administrative support.

4.  As compared to other occupations, careers in science, technology, engineering, and math have
    a.  fewer job openings.
    b.  higher median wages.
    c.  decreased opportunity in the future.

5.  Advances in technology will lead to increased opportunity in
    a.  sales.
    b.  manufacturing.
    c.  business and scientific services.

**How did you do on the quiz? Check your answers: 1. b, 2. c, 3. a, 4. b, 5. c**

# Work Skills for the 21st Century

Because of rapid changes in technology, college students of today may be preparing for jobs that do not exist right now. After graduation, many college students find employment that is not even related to their college majors. One researcher found that 48 percent of college graduates find employment in fields not related to their college majors.[19] More important than one's college major are the general skills learned in college that prepare students for the future.

To define skills needed in the future workplace, the U.S. Secretary of Labor created the Secretary's Commission on Achieving Necessary Skills (SCANS). Based on interviews with employers and educators, the members of the commission outlined foundation skills and workplace competencies needed to succeed in the workplace in the 21st century.[20] The following skills apply to all occupations in all fields and will help you to become a successful employee, regardless of your major. As you read through these skills, think about your competency in these areas.

## Foundation Skills

### Basic Skills

- Reading
- Writing
- Basic arithmetic
- Higher-level mathematics
- Listening
- Speaking

### Thinking Skills

- Creative thinking
- Decision making
- Problem solving
- Mental visualization
- Knowing how to learn
- Reasoning

### Personal Qualities

- Responsibility
- Self-esteem
- Sociability
- Self-management
- Integrity/honesty

## Workplace Competencies

The following are some workplace competencies required to be successful in all well-paying jobs. The successful employee:

- can manage resources such as time, money, materials, and human resources;
- has good interpersonal skills and can participate as a member of a team, teach others, serve clients and customers, exercise leadership, negotiate workable solutions, and work with diverse individuals;
- can learn new information on the job and use computers to acquire, organize, analyze, and communicate information;
- works within the system, monitors and corrects performance, and improves the system as needed;
- uses technology to produce the desired results.

Because the workplace is changing, these skills may be more important than the background acquired through a college major. Work to develop these skills and you will be prepared for whatever lies ahead.

Developing your job skills can prepare you for whatever lies ahead. The TruTalent Skills assessment included in this textbook helps you to identify your highest skills and connect them to majors and careers. This assessment also has suggestions for improving your skills. Skills assessed include critical thinking, conscientiousness, leadership, socio-emotional factors, and creativity.

## Journal Entry

Look at the results of your TruTalent Skills assessment. List your top five skills, along with a brief definition of each one.

**3**

> "The supreme accomplishment is to blur the line between work and play."
> ARNOLD TOYNBEE

# How to Research Your Career

After you have assessed your personality, interests, values, and talents, the next step is to learn about the world of work. If you can match your personal strengths to the world of work, you can find work that is interesting and you can excel in it. To learn about the world of work, you will need to research possible careers. This includes reading career descriptions and investigating career outlooks, salaries, and educational requirements.

> "Starting out to make money is the greatest mistake in life. Do what you feel you have a flair for doing, and if you are good enough at it, the money will come."
> GREER GARSON

## Career Descriptions

The career description tells you about the nature of the work, working conditions, employment, training, qualifications, advancement, job outlook, earnings, and related occupations. The two best sources of job descriptions are the *Occupational Outlook Handbook* and *Occupational Outlook Quarterly*. The *Handbook*, published by the Bureau of Labor Statistics, is like an encyclopedia of careers. You can search alphabetically by career or by career cluster.

The *Occupational Outlook Quarterly* is a periodical with up-to-date articles on new and emerging occupations, training opportunities, salary trends, and new studies from the Bureau of Labor Statistics. You can find these resources in a public or school library, at a college career center, or on the *College Success Website* at http://www.collegesuccess1.com/Links9Career.htm.

## Career Outlook

It is especially important to know about the career outlook of an occupation you are considering. Career outlook includes salary and availability of employment. How much does the occupation pay? Will the occupation exist in the future, and will there be employment opportunities? Of course, you will want to prepare yourself for careers that pay well and have future employment opportunities.

© IQONCEPT/SHUTTERSTOCK.COM

You can find information about career outlooks in the sources listed above, current periodicals, and materials from the Bureau of Labor Statistics. The following table, for example, lists the fastest-growing occupations, occupations with the highest salaries, and occupations with the largest job growth. Information from the Bureau of Labor Statistics is also available online.

## Employment Projections 2019-29

| 10 Fastest Growing Occupations[21] | 10 Industries with the Largest Wage and Salary Growth[22] | 10 Occupations with the Largest Numerical Job Growth[23] |
|---|---|---|
| Wind turbine service technicians | Leisure and hospitality | Nurse practitioners |
| Nurse Practitioners | State and Local Government | Home health care aides |
| Solar photovoltaic installers | Construction | Medical and health managers |
| Occupational therapy assistants | Retail trade | Cooks, restaurant |
| Statisticians | Wholesale trade | Substance abuse and mental health counselors |
| Home health care aides | Health care and social assistance | Animal caretakers |
| Physical therapy assistants | Professional and business services | Software developers |
| Medical managers | Educational services | Medical assistants |
| Physician assistants | Financial activities | Market and research analysts |
| Information security analysts | Hospitals | Social and human service assistants |

## Journal
### Entry

Go to the *Occupational Outlook Handbook* at http://www.bls.gov/ooh/. Choose one career and write a one-sentence description of the career, list the median salary, and report on the job outlook.

4

# Planning Your Education

Once you have assessed your personal characteristics and researched your career options, it is important to plan your education. If you have a plan, you will be able to finish your education more quickly and avoid taking unnecessary classes. You can begin work on your educational plan by following the steps below. After you have done some work on your plan, visit your college counselor or advisor to make sure that your plan is appropriate.

# Activity

## Steps in Planning Your Education

_____ 1. **Take your college entrance or assessment tests before you apply to colleges.** Most colleges require the Scholastic Aptitude Test (SAT) or their own local placement tests in order for you to be admitted. You can find information about these tests at your high school or college counseling center or online at http://www.ets.org/ or http://cbweb1.collegeboard.org/index.html. If you are attending a community college, check the college website, admissions office, or counseling office to see what placement exams are required.

_____ 2. **Take English the first semester, and continue each semester until your English requirement is complete.** English courses provide the foundation for further college study. Your SAT or college placement test will determine what level of English you need to take. As a general rule, community colleges require one semester of college-level English. Four-year colleges and universities generally require two semesters or three quarters of college-level English. If your placement scores are low, you may be required to take review courses first.

_____ 3. **Start your math classes early, preferably in the first semester or quarter.** Many high-paying careers require a long series of math classes, particularly those in the sciences, engineering, and business. If you delay taking math courses until later, you may limit your career options and extend your time in college. Take the required math courses each semester until you have finished your requirements. Having a gap between math courses will make future courses more difficult.

_____ 4. **Take the required general education courses.** Find out what your college requires for general education and put these classes on your plan. You will find this information in the college catalog. Be careful to select the correct general education plan. At community colleges, there are different plans for transfer and associate's degree students. At a university, there may be different plans for different colleges within the university. Check with a college counselor or advisor to make sure you have the correct plan.

_____ 5. **Prepare for your major.** Consult your college catalog to see what courses are required for your major. If you are undecided on a major, take the general education courses and start working on a decision about your major. If you are interested in the sciences or engineering, start work on math in the first semester. Start on your major requirements as soon as possible so that you do not delay your graduation.

_____ 6. **Check prerequisites.** A prerequisite is a course that is required before taking a higher-level course. The college catalog lists courses offered and includes prerequisites. Most colleges will

_____ not let you register for a course for which you do not have the prerequisite. It is also difficult to succeed in an advanced course without taking the prerequisite first.

_____ 7.   **Make an educational plan.** The educational plan includes all the courses you will need to graduate. Again, use the college catalog as your guide.

_____ 8.   **Check your plan.** See your college counselor or advisor to check your plan. He or she can save you from taking classes that you do not need and help you to graduate in the minimum amount of time.

# Making Good Decisions

Knowing how to make a good decision about your career and important life events is very important to your future, as this short poem by J. Wooden sums up:

> *There is a choice you have to make,*
> *In everything you do.*
> *And you must always keep in mind,*
> *The choice you make, makes you.*[24]

Sometimes people end up in a career because they simply seized an opportunity for employment. A good job becomes available and they happen to be in the right place at the right time. Sometimes people end up in a career because it is familiar to them, because it is a job held by a member of the family or a friend in the community. Sometimes people end up in a career because of economic necessity. The job pays well and they need the money. These careers are the result of chance circumstances. Sometimes they turn out well, and sometimes they turn out miserably.

> "Think not of yourself as the architect of your career but as the sculptor. Expect to have a lot of hard hammering, chiseling, scraping and polishing."
> B.C. FORBES

Whether you are male or female, married or single, you will spend a great deal of your life working. By doing some careful thinking and planning about your career, you can improve your chances of success and happiness. Use the following steps to do some careful decision making about your career. Although you are the person who needs to make the decision about a career, you can get help from your college career center or your college counselor or advisor.

## Steps in Making a Career Decision

1.  Begin with self-assessment.
    - What is your personality type?
    - What are your interests?
    - What are your talents, gifts, and strengths?
    - What are your values?
    - What lifestyle do you prefer?

2.  Explore your options.
    - What careers match your personal characteristics?

3. **Research your career options.**
   - Read the job description.
   - Investigate the career outlook.
   - What is the salary?
   - What training and education is required?
   - Speak with an advisor, counselor, or person involved in the career that interests you.
   - Choose a career or general career area that matches your personal characteristics.

4. **Plan your education to match your career goal.**
   - Try out courses in your area of interest.
   - Start your general education if you need more time to decide on a major.
   - Try an internship or part-time job in your area of interest.

5. **Make a commitment to take action and follow through with your plan.**

6. **Evaluate.**
   - Do you like the courses you are taking?
   - Are you doing well in the courses?
   - Continue research if necessary.

7. **Refine your plan.**
   - Make your plan more specific to aim for a particular career.
   - Select the college major that is best for you.

8. **Change your plan if it is not working.**
   - Go back to the self-assessment step.

> "Find a job you like and add five days to every week."
>
> H. JACKSON BROWNE

## The Decision-Making Process

- **Dependent decisions.** Different kinds of decisions are appropriate in different situations. When you make a dependent decision, you depend on someone else to make the decision for you. The dependent decision was probably the first kind of decision that you ever made. When your parents told you what to do as a child, you were making a dependent decision. As an adult, you make a dependent decision when your doctor tells you what medication to take for an illness or when your stockbroker tells you what stock you should purchase. Dependent decisions are easy to make and require little thought. Making a dependent decision saves time and energy.

  The dependent decision, however, has some disadvantages. You may not like the outcome of the decision. The medication that your doctor prescribes may have unpleasant side effects. The stock that you purchased may go down in value. When students ask a counselor to recommend a major or a career, they are making a dependent decision. When the decision does not work, they blame the counselor. Even if the dependent decision does have good results, you may become dependent on others to continue making decisions for you. Dependent decisions do work in certain situations, but they do not give you as much control over your own life.

- **Intuitive decisions.** Intuitive decisions are based on intuition or a gut feeling about what is the best course of action. Intuitive decisions can be made quickly and are useful in dealing with emergencies. If I see a car heading on a collision path toward me, I have to swerve quickly to the right or left. I do not have time to ask someone else what to do or think much about the alternatives. Another example of an intuitive decision is in gambling. If I am trying to decide whether to bet a dollar on red or black, I rely on my gut feeling to make a choice. Intuitive decisions may work out or they may not. You could make a mistake and swerve the wrong way as the car approaches or you could lose your money in gambling.

- **Planful decisions.** For important decisions, it is advantageous to use what is called a planful decision. The planful decision is made after carefully weighing the consequences and the pros and cons of the different alternatives. The planful decision-making strategy is particularly useful for such decisions as:

  - What will be my major?
  - What career should I choose?
  - Whom should I marry?

The steps in a planful decision-making process:

1. **State the problem.** When we become aware of a problem, the first step is to state the problem in the simplest way possible. Just stating the problem will help you to clarify the issues.

2. **Consider your values.** What is important to you? What are your hopes and dreams? By keeping your values in mind, you are more likely to make a decision that will make you happy.

3. **What are your talents?** What special skills do you have? How can you make a decision that utilizes these skills?

4. **Gather information.** What information can you find that would be helpful in solving the problem? Look for ideas. Ask other people. Do some research. Gathering information can give you insight into alternatives or possible solutions to the problem.

5. **Generate alternatives.** Based on the information you have gathered, identify some possible solutions to the problem.

6. **Evaluate the pros and cons of each alternative.** List the alternatives and think about the pros and cons of each one. In thinking about the pros and cons, consider your values and talents as well as your future goals.

7. **Select the best alternative.** Choose the alternative that is the best match for your values and helps you to achieve your goals.

8. **Take action.** You put your decision into practice when you take some action on it. Get started!

**Types of Decisions**
- Dependent
- Intuitive
- Planful

"When written in Chinese, the word 'crisis' is composed of two characters; one represents danger and the other represents opportunity."
JOHN F. KENNEDY

# Quiz

1. When you research the career outlook, you find information about
   a. whether the job is done inside or outside.
   b. the job description.
   c. the salary and availability of employment.

2. In planning your education, it is best to
   a. take English and math early.
   b. try out different courses to find out what you like.
   c. arrange a convenient schedule.

3. Because of rapid changes in technology and the job market, it is important to
   a. major in a science field.
   b. major in a health field.
   c. have good skills in reading, math, communication, and critical thinking.

4. If you make a decision based on your "gut feeling," you risk
   a. making a mistake.
   b. making a dependent decision.
   c. making a planned decision.

5. Career decision making includes
   a. waiting until you finish college to begin the process.
   b. sticking to your plan even if it is not working.
   c. researching your career options.

**How did you do on the quiz? Check your answers: 1. c, 2. a, 3. c, 4. a, 5. c**

# Keys to Success

## Life Is a Dangerous Opportunity

Even though we may do our best in planning our career and education, life does not always turn out as planned. Unexpected events happen, putting our life in crisis. The crisis might be loss of employment, divorce, illness, or death of a loved one. How we deal with the crisis events in our lives can have a great impact on our current well-being and the future.

The Chinese word for crisis has two characters: one character represents danger and the other represents opportunity. Every crisis has the danger of loss of something important and the resulting emotions of frustration, sorrow, and grief. But every crisis also has an opportunity. Sometimes it is difficult to see the opportunity because we are overwhelmed by the danger. A crisis, however, can provide an impetus for change and growth. A crisis forces us to look inside ourselves to find capabilities that have always been there, although we did not know it. If life goes too smoothly, there is no motivation to change. If we get too comfortable, we stop growing. There is no testing of our capabilities. We stay in the same patterns.

To find the opportunity in a crisis, focus on what is possible in the situation. Every adversity has the seed of a greater benefit or possibility. Expect things to work out well. Expect success. To deal with negative emotions, consider that feelings are not simply a result of what happens to us, but of our interpretation of events. If we focus on the danger, we cannot see the possibilities.

As a practical application, consider the example of someone who has just lost a job. John had worked as a construction worker for nearly 10 years when he injured his back. His doctor told him that he would no longer be able to do physical labor. John was 30 years old and had two children and large house and truck payments. He was having difficulty finding a job that paid as well as his construction job, and was suffering from many negative emotions resulting from his loss of employment.

John decided that he would have to use his brain rather than his back. As soon as he was up and moving, he started taking some general education courses at the local college. He assessed his skills and identified his strengths. He was a good father and communicated well with his children. He had wanted to go to college, but got married early and started to work in construction instead. John decided that he would really enjoy being a marriage and family counselor. It would mean getting a bachelor's and a master's degree, which would take five or more years.

John began to search for a way to accomplish this new goal. He first tackled the financial problems. He investigated vocational rehabilitation, veteran's benefits, financial aid, and scholarships. He sold his house and his truck. His wife took a part-time job. He worked out a careful budget. He began to work toward his new goal with a high degree of motivation and self-satisfaction. He had found a new opportunity.

© SHUTTER_M/SHUTTERSTOCK.COM

"When written in Chinese, the word 'crisis' is composed of two characters; one represents danger and the other represents opportunity."
JOHN F. KENNEDY

**Journal Entry**

At times in life, you may face a crisis or setback which causes an unexpected change in plans. If you think positively about the situation, you can think of some new opportunities for the future. This situation is called a dangerous opportunity. Describe a dangerous opportunity you have faced in your life. What were the dangers and what opportunities did you find?

5

> "Life is not about waiting for the storms to pass . . . it's about learning how to dance in the rain."
>
> VIVIAN GREENE

## JOURNAL ENTRIES
## PLANNING YOUR CAREER AND EDUCATION

Go to http://www.collegesuccess1.com/JournalEntries.htm for Word files of the Journal Entries.

## SUCCESS
## over the Internet

**Visit the *College Success Website* at http://www.collegesuccess1.com/**

The *College Success Website* is continually updated with new topics and links to the material presented in this chapter. Topics include:

- Future trends
- Planning your major
- Job descriptions
- Career outlooks
- Career information
- Salary
- Interests
- Self-assessment
- Exploring careers
- Hot jobs for the future
- Profiles of successful people
- The personal side of work
- Using the Internet for a job search
- Job openings
- Decision making

Contact your instructor if you have any problems in accessing the *College Success Website*.

## Notes

1. Michael T. Robinson, "Top Jobs for the Future," from www.careerplanner.com, 2004.
2. Gail Sheehy, *New Passages* (New York: Random House, 1995), 34.
3. Jeff Giles, "Generalization X," *Newsweek*, June 6, 1994.
4. Jane Bryant Quinn, "The Luck of the Xers, Comeback Kids: Young People Will Live Better Than They Think," *Newsweek*, 6 June 1994, 66–67.
5. Ellen Neuborne, http://www.businessweek.com, 1999.
6. Claudia Smith Brison, http://www.thestate.com, 14 July 2002.

7.  Neil Howe and William Strauss, *Millennials Rising: The Next Great Generation* (New York: Vintage Books, 2000):

8.  *USA Today*, "After Gen X, Millennials, What Should Next Generation Be?" by Bruce Horovitz, May 24, 2012.

9.  *USA Today*, "After Gen X, Millennials, What Should Next Generation Be?" by Bruce Horovitz, May 24, 2012. US Census Bureau, "State and County QuickFacts 2012", http://quickfacts.census. gov/qfd/states/00000.html

10. "The First Generation of the Twenty First Century, an Introduction to the Pluralist Generation" by Magid Generational Strategies, April 30, 2012 from http://magid. com/ sites/default/files/pdf/MagidPluralistGenerationWhitepaper.pdf

11. Neuborne, www.businessweek.com, 1999.

12. Daniel Lavelle, "Move Over, Millennials and GenZ-Here Comes Generation Alpha," retrieved from https://www.theguardian.com/society/short-cuts/2019/jan/04/move-over-millennials-and-gen-z-here-comes-generation-alpha, September 2020.

13. Mark McCrindle and Ashley Fell, "Understanding the Impact of Covid-19 on the Emerging Generations," May 2020, https://mccrindle.com.au/wp-content/uploads/COVID19-Emerging-Generations-Report.pdf.

14. Shubhangi Srinivasan, "15 Employment Trends Shaping the Future of Jobs," December 7, 2019, https://www.feedough.com/employment-trends-2019/.

15. Ibid.

16. US Bureau of Labor Statistics, "Employment in Stem Occupations," last modified September 1, 2020, https://www.bls.gov/emp/tables/stem-employment.htm.

17. US Bureau of Labor Statistics, "Employment Projections: 2019–2029 Summary," September 1, 2020, https://www.bls.gov/news.release/ecopro.nr0.htm.

18. US Bureau of Labor Statistics, "Employment Projections: 2019–2029 Summary," September 1, 2020, https://www.bls.gov/news.release/ecopro.nr0.htm.

19. T.J. Grites, "Being 'Undecided' Could Be the Best Decision They Could Make," *School Counselor* 29 (1981): 41-46.

20. Secretary's Commission on Achieving Necessary Skills (SCANS), *Learning a Living: A Blueprint for High Performance* (Washington, DC: U.S. Department of Labor, 1991).

21. "Fastest Growing Occupations," Bureau of Labor Statistics, last modified September 1, 2020, https://www.bls.gov/ooh/fastest-growing.htm

22. "Industries with the Largest Wage and Salary Employment Growth and Declines," Bureau of Labor Statistics, last modified September 1, 2020, https://www.bls.gov/ooh/fastest-growing.htm

23. "Occupations with the Most Job Growth," Bureau of Labor Statistics, last modified September 1, 2020, https://www.bls.gov/emp/tables/occupations-most-job-growth.htm

24. Quoted in Rob Gilbert, ed., *Bits and Pieces*, November 4, 1999.

# RATE YOUR SKILLS FOR SUCCESS IN THE WORKPLACE

Read each statement relating to skills needed for success in the workplace. Use the following scale to rate your competencies:

5 = Excellent   4 = Very good   3 = Average   2 = Needs improvement   1 = Need to develop

_____ 1.  I have good reading skills. I can locate information I need to read and understand and interpret it. I can pick out the main idea and judge the accuracy of the information.

_____ 2.  I have good writing skills. I can communicate thoughts, ideas, and information in writing. I know how to edit and revise my writing and use correct spelling, punctuation, and grammar.

_____ 3.  I am good at arithmetic. I can perform basic computations using whole numbers and percentages. I can make reasonable estimates without a calculator and can read tables, graphs, and charts.

_____ 4.  I am good at mathematics. I can use a variety of mathematical techniques including statistics to predict the occurrence of events.

_____ 5.  I am good at speaking. I can organize my ideas and participate in discussions and group presentations. I speak clearly and am a good listener. I ask questions to obtain feedback when needed.

_____ 6.  I am a creative thinker. I can come up with new ideas and unusual connections. I can imagine new possibilities and combine ideas in new ways.

_____ 7.  I make good decisions. I can specify goals and constraints, generate alternatives, consider risks, and evaluate alternatives.

_____ 8.  I am good at solving problems. I can see when a problem exists, identify the reasons for the problem, and devise a plan of action for solving the problem.

_____ 9.  I am good at mental visualization. I can see things in my mind's eye. Examples include building a project from a blueprint or imagining the taste of a recipe from reading it.

_____ 10.  I know how to learn new information. I am aware of my learning style and can use learning strategies to obtain new knowledge.

_____ 11.  I am good at reasoning. I can use logic to draw conclusions and apply rules and principles to new situations.

_____ 12.  I am a responsible person. I work toward accomplishing goals, set high standards, and pay attention to details. I usually accomplish tasks on time.

_____ 13.  I have high self-esteem. I believe in my self-worth and maintain a positive view of myself.

_____ 14.  I am sociable, understanding, friendly, adaptable, polite, and relate well to others.

_____ 15. I am good at self-management. I know my background, skills, and abilities and set realistic goals for myself. I monitor my progress toward completing my goals and complete them.

_____ 16. I practice integrity and honesty. I recognize when I am faced with a decision that involves ethics and choose ethical behavior.

_____ 17. I am good at managing my time. I set goals, prioritize, and follow schedules to complete tasks on time.

_____ 18. I manage money well. I know how to use and prepare a budget and keep records, making adjustments when necessary.

_____ 19. I can manage material and resources. I can store and distribute materials, supplies, parts, equipment, space, or products.

_____ 20. I can participate as a member of a team. I can work cooperatively with others and contribute to group efforts.

_____ 21. I can teach others. I can help others to learn needed knowledge and skills.

_____ 22. I can exercise leadership. I know how to communicate, encourage, persuade, and motivate individuals.

_____ 23. I am a good negotiator. I can work toward an agreement and resolve divergent interests.

_____ 24. I can work with men and women from a variety of ethnic, social, or educational backgrounds.

_____ 25. I can acquire and evaluate information. I can identify a need for information and find the information I need.

_____ 26. I can organize and maintain information. I can find written or computerized information.

_____ 27. I can use computers to process information.

_____ 28. I have an understanding of social, organizational, and technological systems and can operate effectively in these systems.

_____ 29. I can improve the design of a system to improve the quality of products and services.

_____ 30. I can use machines and computers to accomplish the desired task.

_____ Total

Score your skills for success in the workplace.

| | |
|---|---|
| 150–121 | Excellent |
| 120–91 | Very good |
| 90–61 | Average |
| Below 60 | Need improvement |

From the previous list of workplace skills, make a list of five of your strong points. What do you do well?

From the list of workplace skills, make a list of areas you need to improve.

# THE PLANFUL DECISION STRATEGY

Read the following scenario describing a college student in a problem situation. Then, answer the questions that follow to practice the planful decision strategy. You may want to do this as a group activity with other students in the class.

Rhonda is an 18-year-old student who is trying to decide on her major. She was a good student in high school, earning a 3.4 grade point average. Her best subjects were English and American history. She struggled with math and science but still earned good grades in these subjects. While in high school, she enjoyed being on the debate team and organizing the African American Club. This club was active in writing letters to the editor and became involved in supporting a local candidate for city council.

Rhonda is considering majoring in political science and has dreams of eventually going to law school. Rhonda likes being politically involved and advocating for different social causes. The highlight of her life in high school was when she organized students to speak to the city council about installing a traffic light in front of the school after a student was killed trying to cross the street. The light was installed during her senior year.

Rhonda's family has always been supportive, and she values her family life and the close relationships in the family. She comes from a middle-income family that is struggling to pay for her college education. Getting a bachelor's degree in political science and going to law school would take seven years and be very expensive. There is no law school in town, so Rhonda would have to move away from home to attend school.

Rhonda's parents have suggested that she consider becoming a nurse and attending the local nursing college. Rhonda could finish a bachelor's degree in nursing in four years and could begin working part-time as a nurse's aide in a short time. A cousin in the family became a nurse and found a job easily and is now earning a good income. The cousin arranged for Rhonda to volunteer this summer at the hospital where she works. Rhonda enjoys helping people at the hospital. Rhonda is trying to decide on her major. What should she do?

1. State the problem.

2. Describe Rhonda's values, hopes, and dreams.

3. What special interests, talents, or aptitudes does she have?

4. What further information would be helpful to Rhonda in making her decision?

5. What are the alternatives and the pros and cons of each?

| Alternative 1 | |
|---|---|
| Pros: | Cons: |
| | |

| Alternative 2 | |
|---|---|
| Pros: | Cons: |
| | |

| Alternative 3 (be creative!) | |
|---|---|
| Pros: | Cons: |
| | |

6. Only Rhonda can choose what is best for her. If you were Rhonda, what would you do and why? Use a separate piece of paper, if necessary, to write your answer.

# Updated Job Search Strategies

# 6

## Learning

## OBJECTIVES

Read to answer these key questions:

- How can I increase my chances for employment after graduation?

- What are some tips for writing my resume and cover letter?

- How do I establish my own personal brand for marketing myself online?

- What are some online tools that can help me find a job?

- How can I prepare for the job interview?

- What is an informational interview?

- What are some options for starting my own business?

- How do I set up a job search plan and begin taking action?

> "Anything you really want, you can attain, if you really go after it."
> WAYNE DYER

While in college, you can increase your chances of obtaining employment after graduation by using Career Services at your college, volunteering, doing internships, and working part time. Get started by writing your resume and cover letter. Establish your personal brand by assessing your personal strengths and using social media to market yourself to potential employers. Learn about some online tools for searching for that ideal job as well as how to be successful on the interview. Alternatively you may want to consider starting your own business. The most important last step is taking action on your job search plan.

# Increasing Your Chances for Employment

## Using Your College Career Services

Your College Career Services can assist you in your career planning as well as finding employment, internships, and volunteer opportunities while in college and after graduation. Here are some typical career services:

- Career assessment and counseling
- Career fairs
- Career library
- Employment information
- Job postings
- Job search resources
- Majors and related careers
- Resume assistance
- Interview assistance
- Reference service
- Opportunities for volunteering, internships, and work or study abroad

## Volunteering

Volunteering not only helps your community, but it can help your job search in many ways:

- Volunteering improves your confidence and self-worth and gives you a sense of accomplishment. It helps you to develop leadership skills.
- You can add contacts to your network. Most people find jobs through personal and professional contacts.
- If you have little job experience, volunteering looks good on your resume.
- You can learn new skills by volunteering.
- Volunteering is a way to try out a career to see if you like it. For example, if you are thinking about becoming a teacher, volunteer at a school to gain some first-hand experience and to see if teaching is really the career for you.

- Learn about job opportunities while volunteering.
- Ask for recommendations or endorsements after you have finished your volunteer position.

To find a volunteer position, start with Career Services at your college. This office often has volunteer positions related to the majors at their college. You can also research volunteer positions online at volunteermatch.com, which matches your interests to positions available in your community.

## Internships

The purpose of an internship is to learn job skills and increase your networking possibilities while you are in college. Internships are often low paid or unpaid positions in a company or organization that is in your area of career interest. Some internships can lead to jobs when you finish college or at least look good on your resume. Colleges set up internships with local companies and may even offer you college credit for them. Begin by contacting Career Services at your college. This office often sets up internships to match the majors at the college. You can also use http://www.internships.com/ to begin an Internet search, or join LinkedIn and click on Jobs for Students and Recent Graduates to find opportunities in your area. Another possibility is contacting companies matching your interests and asking them if they have any internship possibilities.

A good internship is one in which you have the opportunity to experience hands-on learning and gain knowledge in the field, which can be valuable in your future career. Often interns shadow employees to learn about their jobs. Internships vary in quality, with the least valuable ones having interns doing busy work with little opportunity to learn valuable skills for the future. It is best to start by figuring out the careers you would like to explore and then carefully investigating what you will be doing as an intern to make sure it is worth your time.

## Working While in College

About 80 percent of students work while in college and this employment provides many advantages. It can provide needed income and valuable job experience as well as increased social contacts that can be useful in the future. This work looks good on your resume and can be used for future references. It is also a way of limiting debt by reducing the money you have to borrow for college. Research has shown that students who work 10–15 hours a week are more likely to persist and finish their college degrees. Working while in colleges requires time management skills that can be useful in future employment. Having to plan your study time and work can even result in higher grades, since you will have to schedule your study time and will be more focused on getting your school work done.[1]

However, students are often tempted to work more than the recommended amount, which results in increased stress as they try to balance the demands of employment, study, and social life. This is likely to result in longer time for degree completion or may even interfere with attaining a degree. If you find it necessary to work more than the recommended amount, consider going to college part time.

## Journal Entry

What are some ways you can increase your chances of employment while in college? Consider volunteering, internships, or work opportunities.

**1**

## Get Started with a Resume and Cover Letter

*"The nearest to perfection that most people come is when filling out an employment application."*
SOURCE UNKNOWN

Your resume is important in establishing a good first impression and provides the basic content for job seeking social media sites such as LinkedIn and Facebook. A resume is a snapshot of your education and experience. It is generally one page in length. You will need a resume to apply for scholarships, part-time jobs, or find a position after you graduate. Start with a file of information you can use to create your resume. Keep your resume on file in your computer or on your flash drive so that you can revise it or post it online as needed. Your college career center will likely have resume building software and can assist you in creating and revising your resume.

A resume includes the following basic components:

- Contact information: your name, address, telephone number, and email address

- A brief statement of your career objective
- A summary of your education:
  - Names and locations of schools
  - Dates of attendance
  - Diplomas or degrees received
- A summary of your work and/or volunteer experience
- If you have little directly related work experience, a list of courses you have taken that would help the employer understand your skills for employment
- Special skills, honors, awards, or achievements
- References (people who can recommend you for a job or scholarship)

There is no one best way to write a resume, but here are some helpful tips:

- Begin your resume with your contact information. Make sure that your email is professional. Consider creating a new email for job seeking purposes. Your email should include your first and last name.
- In the job history section, include brief statements about job tasks, including what you did to make your company better. It is helpful to look for key words in the job announcement and make sure these key words are in your resume.
- List your present or most recent job first and work back chronologically.
- If you are just graduating from college and have little work experience, put the education section first along with related coursework.
- Keep in mind that the average resume gets read in 10 seconds. Make sure your resume is organized and brief. Bold those ideas that you want to highlight.
- Do not include personal information or photos.

- Carefully proofread your resume to make sure it has no errors. It is a good idea to have someone else review it also.
- Store your resume on your computer so that you can update it regularly and have it available to post online.

It is easy to upload your content to resume templates online. Here are some resume template sites:

Choose your template from a variety of examples and then create or upload your content.
http://www.myperfectresume.com/

This site has 114 templates depending on your experience and career. You can upload your current resume into a suggested template and add their suggested improvements.
http://www.resume-now.com/

Ask for a letter of reference from your current supervisor at work or someone in a position to recommend you, such as a college professor or community member. Ask the person to address the letter "To Whom It May Concern" so that you can use the letter many times. If the person is on LinkedIn, ask him or her for an endorsement. The person recommending you should comment on your work habits, skills, and personal qualities. If appropriate, offer to write the letter yourself and then the person can edit it or send it as is. This often helps people who would like to recommend you, but are very busy. If you wait until you graduate to obtain letters of reference, potential recommenders may no longer be there or may not remember who you are. Always ask if you can use a person's name as a reference. When you are applying for a job and references are requested, phone the persons who have agreed to recommend you and let them know to expect a call.

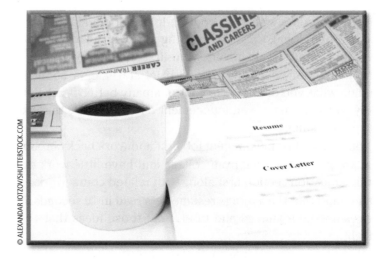

© ALEXANDAR IOTZOV/SHUTTERSTOCK.COM

While most resumes are shared online, if you need a printed copy, print your resume so that it looks professional. Use a good quality white, tan, or gray paper. It is a good idea to take a printed copy of your resume to an interview.

When you respond to job announcements, you may be asked to send a cover letter with your resume attached. Address your letter to a specific person at the company or organization and spell the name correctly. You can call the personnel office to obtain this information. The purpose of the cover letter is to state your interest in the job, highlight your qualifications, and get the employer to read your resume and call you for an interview. The cover letter should be brief and to the point. Include the following items:

> "A major reason many Americans still struggle to find meaningful work is because they are using tactics from the 1990s and early 2000s. The future for employment is now here . . . and it's online."
>
> MATT KEENER

- State the job you are interested in and how you heard about the opening.
- Briefly state how your education and experience would be assets to the company.
- Ask for an interview and tell the employer how you can be contacted.
- Attach your resume.
- Your cover letter is the first contact you have with the employer. Make it neat and free from errors. Use spell check and grammar check, read it over again, and have someone else check it for you.

Select templates and view samples of cover letters online at http://www.cover-letter-now.com/

# Quiz

## Getting Started

1. While attending college, you can gain valuable experience by working, but it is recommended that if you are a full-time student, you work no more than ___ hours per week.

   a. 30–35
   b. 10–15
   c. 5–10

2. A resume is generally _____ page(s) in length.

   a. four
   b. one
   c. two

3. Begin your resume with your

   a. job objective.
   b. educational history.
   c. contact information.

4. To format your resume, use

   a. an online template.
   b. an outline.
   c. bold headings.

5. The cover letter

   a. contains a brief statement of how your qualifications would be an asset to the company.
   b. includes a detailed list of your education and experience.
   c. does not include a request for an interview.

**How did you do on the quiz? Check your answers: 1. b, 2. b, 3. c, 4. a, 5. a**

# Establishing Your Personal Brand Online

Personal branding is the process by which we market ourselves to others. It is an important concept that has been used to sell products and services. Through the use of social media, you can use this concept to market your strengths to potential employers and to find a satisfying career. Throughout this textbook you have been challenged to become more aware of these personal strengths that can be used to create your own personal brand. Here are the steps for establishing your personal brand and marketing yourself:

> "Everyone should find something they love doing. Then work isn't work. It's a part of themselves. Of who they are."
>
> PAUL MCAULEY

## Define Your Brand

The first step in marketing yourself is to define your personal brand. What are your passions, goals, and personal strengths and how can they be used in the job market? Review the assessments in this textbook and write a brief description of your personal brand along with a brief job title. A few examples of a personal brand include financial expert, entrepreneur, educator, consultant, engineer, and personal trainer.

## Manage Your Online Presence

Most employers do online searches to find employees and to find information on job candidates before the interview. Make sure that your online presence is a professional one that you would want an employer to see. Make sure that your email address is a professional one or consider setting up an account for job seeking. Google your name and see what information a potential employer can find about you. Take a look at your online sites and make sure that the content is appropriate. Some online content may make it difficult to be hired, including:

- Photos or references to drug or alcohol use or abuse.
- Discriminatory comments on race, religion, or gender.
- Negative comments about previous employers.
- Poor communication skills.

When using Facebook, manage your privacy settings so that no one can see your list of friends, since you can be judged by the company you keep and you have no control over what your friends post. To keep your friends private, specify that no one can tag you in a Facebook photo without your authorization. Be careful about what you put on your front page, since it is the most visible page.

## Set up a Nameplate Website

Take control of your online presence by setting up a nameplate website that defines who you are and directs potential employers to your media sites. On these sites, you can upload your photo, include your biography, list your education, describe your work experience, and provide links to LinkedIn or Facebook. Here are some free sites you can use to set up your nameplate website:

- sites.google.com
- wordpress.org
- about.me
- zerply.com
- re.vu

# Using Online Tools

At the present time, LinkedIn, Facebook, and Indeed.com are the most common sites used by employers to research job candidates. Invest some of your time setting up accounts at these sites.

## LinkedIn

LinkedIn is a directory of professionals and companies used for job searching, networking, and hiring. Many employers use LinkedIn profiles to search for potential employees. This profile is similar to a resume and includes your education and job experience. Make sure that your profile is complete and well written since it represents who you are online. Since recruiting software is used to search through profiles, use key words in your resume that relate to your desired job. Key words include job requirements, experience, software competencies, education, and previous employers. To find key words, take a look at job listings in your area of interest and expertise and include the words in your profile. It is helpful to include recommendations and endorsements that you can request from other contacts on LinkedIn. Personalize your profile by uploading a photo. Use a current photo and dress appropriately for the type of job you are seeking.

LinkedIn is also a job search tool in which you can search for and apply for jobs within the site. The job listings page allows you to search for jobs by location, industry, company, job function, level or position, employer, or key words. The site can also be used for networking. As you link to others, they can refer you to jobs open at their site. Maintaining a large network is job security, because you can use it for job advancement or to find a new job in the future. You can join groups of other professionals in your area of expertise to receive notices about job openings in your area of interest. Use the status update function to let your contacts know that you are looking for a job.

When you find a specific job listing in which you are interested, you will have the option to apply within LinkedIn or you will be directed to the company website where you will need to create an account. The site also provides company profiles to help you to find the job that best matches your qualifications and help you with information useful for interviewing.

© LUKASZ STEFANSKI/SHUTTERSTOCK.COM

## Facebook

Facebook is a social network that can be useful in finding a job. The first step in using your Facebook account to find a job is to clean up your profile to make sure that it does not contain any detrimental content. The next step is to post a status update to let your friends know that you are looking for a job and to ask if they know about any job openings.

Use Facebook as a marketing tool. Post samples or links to your work online. If you are a photographer, post some of your photos online. If you are a writer, post links to material you have written. Keep your materials up to date so that prospective employers can see your best and most recent work. If your chosen company has a public Facebook page, you can show your passion, knowledge, and interest for your dream job by participating in discussion boards that can showcase your expertise. You can "like" the company on Facebook and receive news, information, and job openings from them. You can join or create groups on Facebook to discuss your area of interest. In this way, you may be considered for a job before it is posted.

Use Facebook's Marketplace app to search for jobs. Just click on Jobs in Marketplace and enter the job in which you are interested. It contains information about job openings and links to sites with job applications. Facebook also has an app called Social Jobs that allows you to search for jobs.

## Indeed.com

Notice that the career assessments used in this textbook link your personal strengths and interests to matching careers. These careers are linked to Indeed.com which shows current job openings in your location and area of interest.

## Journal
### Entry
| What steps can you take to establish or improve your personal brand? | **2** |

## Classified Ads

One of the most traditional ways to find a job is by looking at classified ads in your local newspaper. These ads are available in online editions of newspapers and are searchable by date, category, keyword, and location. CareerBuilder.com, one of the leading job search sites, contains classified ads from many local and national newspapers as well as employer websites. You can search this site by key word, date, location, or zip code and create an alert to have matching job openings emailed to you. With the Advanced Search option, you can search jobs by radius of a certain location, required degree, salary range, and type of employment. Use the Career Builder Job Machine to upload your resume and cover letter.

> "We do not go to work only to earn an income, but to find meaning in our lives. What we do is a large part of what we are."
> ALAN RYAN

## Job Search Engines

Numerous job search engines list current job openings and have information about current trends and salaries. Here are some useful sites:

- http://www.simplyhired.com/
- www.linkup.com/
- indeed.com

## Employment Agencies

An employment agency is a firm hired by the employer to help with finding the right employees for both temporary and permanent jobs. Employers are motivated to use employment agencies because they do the initial screening and interviewing and save the employer time and money. The cost is usually paid by the employer, but it is a good idea to find out up front if there is any cost to you. Generally the agency works on a contingency basis and does not get paid until they find suitable employees for the job listings. Some private employment agencies do charge for finding you a job and the payment can be a percentage of your first year salary.

The employment agency acts as your advocate and looks for jobs for you. The process begins by submitting a resume and having an interview with the employment agency. The agency will help you with your resume and prepare you for the interview.

## Using Email to Find a Job

You can use email as a tool for finding a job by letting people in your network know that you are looking for a position. You can also target potential employers and ask about job openings. Here are some ideas for using email in your job search:

- Use a separate email account for your job search. The account name should be professional and include your first and last name. Gmail and Yahoo offer free email accounts.
- Write your email like a business letter with complete sentences, good grammar, and clear writing. Check your message for accuracy.
- It is important to include the position for which you are applying in the subject line.

- Copy and paste your cover letter into the email and attach your resume.
- Include an email signature with your contact information that includes your full name, email address, and phone number.
- You can include a link to your LinkedIn profile or nameplate website, such as about.me.

## Journal
## Entry

List some tools that you can use to find a job.

**3**

# The Job Interview

Knowing how to be successful in an interview will help you to get the job that you want. Here are some ideas for being prepared and making a good impression.

- **Learn about the job.**   Before the interview, it is important to research both the company and the job. This research will help you in two ways: you will know if the job is really the one you want and you will have information that will help you to succeed at the interview. If you have taken the time to learn about the company before the interview, you will make a good impression and show that you are really interested in the job. Here are some ways that you can find this information:
    - Visit the company website on the Internet and find out about the company mission and services or products provided. You can find many company profiles on LinkedIn and Facebook.
    - Do any of your friends on Facebook or contacts on LinkedIn work for the company? You can ask for their advice on how to apply for a job. Do any of your family, friends, or teachers know someone who works for the company? If so, you can find out valuable information about the company.
    - The personnel office often has informational brochures that describe the employer.
- **Understand the criteria used in an interview.**   The interviewer represents the company and is looking for the best person to fill the job. It is your job to show the interviewer that you will do a good job. Of course you are interested in salary and benefits, but in order to get hired you must first convince the interviewer that you have something to offer the company. Focus on what you can offer the company based on your education and experience and what you have learned about the company. You may be able to obtain information on salary and benefits from the personnel office before the interview.

    Interviewers look for candidates who show the enthusiasm and commitment necessary to do a good job. They are interested in hiring

> **Tips for a Successful Job Interview**
> - Learn about the job
> - Understand the criteria used in the interview
> - Make a good impression
> - Anticipate interview questions
> - Send a thank you note

someone who can work as part of a team. Think about your education and experience and be prepared to describe your skills and give examples of how you have been successful on the job. Give a realistic and honest description of your work.

- **Make a good impression.**   Here are some suggestions for making a good impression:
  - Dress appropriately for the interview. Look at how the employees of the company dress and then dress a little better. Of course, your attire will vary with the type of job you are seeking. You will dress differently if you are interviewing for a position as manager of a surf shop or an entry-level job in an engineering firm. Wear a conservative, dark colored or neutral suit for most professional positions. Do not wear too much jewelry and remove excess body piercings (unless you are working at a piercing shop). Cover any tattoos if they are not appropriate for the workplace.
  - Relax during the interview. You can relax by preparing in advance. Research the company so you have some familiarity with it. Visualize yourself in the interview room feeling confident about the interview.
  - When you enter the interview room, smile, introduce yourself, and shake hands with the interviewer. If your hands are cold and clammy, go to the restroom before the interview and run warm water over your hands or rub them together.
  - Maintain eye contact with the interviewer and sit up straight. Poor posture or leaning back in your chair could be seen as a lack of confidence or interest in the job.

**Making a Good Impression**

- Dress appropriately
- Relax
- Prepare in advance
- Smile
- Shake hands
- Introduce yourself
- Maintain eye contact
- Sit up straight

© CARTOON RESOURCE/SHUTTERSTOCK.COM

"Was the interview too early for you?"

- **Anticipate the interview questions.** Listen carefully to the interview questions. Ask for clarification of any question you do not understand. Answer the questions concisely and honestly. It helps to anticipate the questions that are likely to be asked and to think about your answers in advance. Generally, be prepared to talk about yourself, your goals, and your reasons for applying for the job. Have a friend ask you the following interview questions and practice answering them. Here are some questions that are typically asked in interviews and some suggestions for answering them:

1.  **What can you tell us about yourself?**
    Think about the job requirements and remember that the interviewer is looking for someone who will do a good job for the company. Talk about your education and experience as it relates to the job. You can put in interesting facts about your life and your hobbies, but keep your answers brief. This question is generally an ice breaker that helps the interviewer get a general picture of you and help you relax.

2.  **Why do you want this job? Why should I hire you?**
    Think about the research you did on this company and several ways that you could benefit the company. A good answer might be, "I have always been good at technical skills and engineering. I am interested in putting these technical skills into practice in your company." A not-so-good answer would be, "I'm interested in making a lot of money and need health insurance."

3.  **Why are you leaving your present job?**
    Instead of saying that the boss was horrible and the working conditions were intolerable (even if this was the case), think of some positive reasons for leaving such as:
    - I am looking for a job that provides challenge and an opportunity for growth.
    - I received my degree and am looking for a job where I can use my education.
    - I had a part-time job to help me through school. I have graduated and am looking for a career.
    - I moved (or the company downsized or went out of business).

    Be careful about discussing problems on your previous job. The interviewers might assume that you were the cause of the problems or that you could not get along with other people.

4.  **What are your strengths and weaknesses?**
    Think about your strengths in relation to the job requirements and be prepared to talk about them during the interview. When asked about your weaknesses, smile and try to turn them into strengths. For example, if you are an introvert, you might say that you are quiet and like to concentrate on your work, but you make an effort to communicate with others

on the job. If you are an extrovert, say that you enjoy talking and working with others, but you are good at time management and get the job done on time. If you are a perfectionist, say that you like to do an excellent job, but you know the importance of meeting deadlines, so you do the best you can in the time available.

5. **Tell us about a difficulty or problem that you solved on the job.**
   Think about some problem that you successfully solved on the job and describe how you did it. Focus on what you accomplished. If the problem was one that dealt with other people, do not focus on blaming or complaining. Focus on your desire to work things out and work well with everyone.

6. **Tell us about one of your achievements on the job.**
   Give examples of projects you have done on the job that have turned out well and projects that gave you a sense of pride and accomplishment.

7. **What do you like best about your work? What do you like least?**
   Think about these questions in advance and use the question about what you like best to highlight your skills for the job. For the question about what you like the least, be honest but express your willingness to do the job that is required.

8. **Are there any questions that you would like to ask?**
   Based on your research on the company, think of some specific questions that show your interest in the company. A good question might be, "Tell me about your company's plans for the future." A not-so-good question would be, "How much vacation do I get?"

9. **Write a thank you note.**
   Express your interest in the job and thank the interviewer. It makes a good impression and causes the interviewer to think about you again.

## Informational Interviewing

The informational interview is an informal conversation useful for finding career information, exploring your career, building your network, or possibly finding future employment. It is not a job interview and the purpose is not to find employment. It is a way to find more personal information about a career you may be considering and to see if you are a good fit for this occupation.

The informational interview differs from the traditional interview in that you are in control and can ask questions about daily job tasks and how they relate to your interests. It is a great way to build your self-confidence and prepare you for an actual job interview. To obtain an informational interview, check your LinkedIn contacts to see if anyone you know is employed in the industry. Ask your friends, family, and employers if they can recommend someone for the interview. You can also work with your college Career Services to see if they have contacts for informational interviews. They often

"All our dreams can come true, if we have the courage to pursue them."
WALT DISNEY

have contacts with college alumni who are willing to speak with students. You can visit websites to identify individuals you would like to interview. Most professionals enjoy helping others who have an interest in their field.

Regard the informational interview as a business appointment and dress the way others dress in this occupation. Make a short appointment (generally 15–30 minutes), state that the purpose of the appointment is to gain career information and advice, and show up on time. You can suggest that the person meet you for coffee (and be sure to pay the bill yourself). Be prepared with a list of questions to ask and to take some brief notes on the information. To begin the interview, give a brief 30 second overview of your career goals and reasons for contacting this person. Remember that the focus of the interview is to find career information. It is best not to ask for a job at this time. If there is a job available and you are a good fit for the job, he or she will likely tell you about it.

It is important to thank the interviewer and then follow up a thank you note or email. Ask the person if he or she is on LinkedIn and if you can request a link online. Bring your resume and hand it to the person at the end of the interview. Do not begin the interview with the resume since you want the focus on career information rather than on yourself.

Here is a sample phone call asking for an informational interview:

*Hello. My name is _____ and I am a student at _____ University. I found your name at your company website. (Or _____ gave me your name and suggested that I contact you.) Although I am not currently looking for a job, I am interested in the field of _____ and would like to learn more about this occupation. Would it be possible to schedule 15–30 minutes of your time to ask a few questions and get your advice on how to enter this field?*

Following is a list of potential interview questions that you can use to keep the conversation going. You probably won't have time to ask all these questions, so choose the ones most that are most personally relevant.

1. What is your job title? What other job titles are commonly used for this position?

2. How did you get this position? What was your career path from entry-level to the position you now have?

3. What are your key job responsibilities? What is the typical day like for you?

4. What skills and education are needed for this job?

5. What are the most valuable courses that you took to prepare you for this job?

6. What are employers looking for (skills, education, personal qualities)?

7. What certificates or degrees are required for this job?

8. What kinds of internships or work experiences are desirable? Are internships available?

9. How does a person obtain this type of employment? How is the job advertised? Is the job market competitive? How can I meet the competition?

10. What are some entry-level positions in this company?

11. What important words should I include on my resume or cover letter?

12. What are the opportunities for advancement?

13. What are some personal characteristics that lead to success on this job?

14. What do you find most satisfying about your job?

15. What are the best and worst things about working in this job? What do you like about your job? Dislike?

16. What stresses you out about your job? What is the most difficult part of your job?

17. What are some of the most important challenges facing your industry today? How will it change in the next 10 years?

18. What is the salary range? What is the potential for advancement?

19. If you were still a college student, what would it be helpful to know about your current job and how to find employment in your field?

20. Can you suggest other sources or persons who could be valuable sources of information for me?

**Journal**
**Entry**

A friend is looking for a job. What advice would you give him or her about the resume and job interview?

**4**

# Starting Your Own Business

One solution to the problem of limited job opportunities is to start your own business. The New Millennial and Generation Z are more than twice as likely as past generations to start their own businesses. They are inspired by Mark Zuckerberg who founded Facebook while he was a sophomore at Harvard University. This new trend is powered by the opportunities provided by Facebook and other social media and the availability of support and funding for entrepreneurs. Websites like GoFundMe, Kickstarter, and Fundable help you obtain funds from friends, family, and contacts. Many colleges offer business plan competitions with startup money for new businesses.[2]

If you are considering the option of starting your own business, here are some steps you may want to consider:

- Use time management to take advantage of some of the flexible time between classes and studying to make plans for your own business.
- Realize that starting your own business requires motivation, hard work, and focus. You will need discipline to balance going to class, studying, and starting your own business.
- Building on a central theme in this textbook, "find your passion," build your skills and find ways you can make money doing something that you enjoy. You can also research small business ideas for college students on the Internet.[3]
- Find an entry-level job or internship in the area of your interest so that you can see how the industry works. Look around and see how things can be improved or how you can help the company make more money.
- Find other motivated students who want to start a business and work with them as a group.

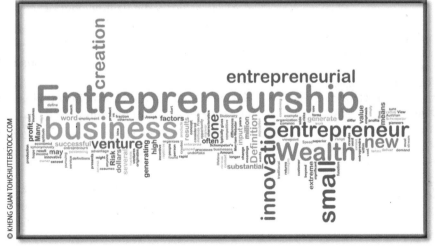

© KHENG GUAN TOH/SHUTTERSTOCK.COM

- Become familiar with social media. Most new businesses started by college students are promoted through Facebook, Twitter, and Instagram.
- Look around for common problems and find solutions. For example, Daniel Vitiello of Texas Tech University had a friend who dropped his iPhone and Daniel was able to fix it. He started an Internet-based iPhone repair business that earned $25,000 a month.[4]
- Take some summer courses in business, marketing, finance, and entrepreneurship.
- Create a business plan with a description, mission, values statement, pricing, financial projections, start-up capital required, and operations timeline.

You can search the Internet for examples of successful student businesses. Here are just a few examples that show how students look for problems and find solutions using their own personal experience:[5]

- Fei Xiao and Anna Sergeeva of the University of Southern California created trueRSVP, which compares the number of people who RSVP to an event to the number who actually attend. This app is useful for event planners.
- Todd Medema of Carnegie Mellon University created AutoRef, which he hopes will make automobile salespersons obsolete. He site has three million cars from 5,000 dealers.
- Brian Silverman of Duke University created Star Toilet Paper, which features ads from local businesses.
- Wesley Zhao of the University of Pennsylvania created FamilyLeaf, a social media site that allows family members to exchange photos.
- Gabrielle Palermo of Arizona State University created G3Box to create cost-effective medical clinics out of recycled shipping containers.
- Kenny Nguyen of Louisiana State University observed that his professors needed help in making their lectures better. He founded Big Fish Presentations, which does design, consultation, and production of commercial video.
- Karina Pikhart of the Massachusetts Institute of Technology created 6Dot, a label maker for blind people.
- Jack McDermott of Tufts University used his own experience with speech therapy to create an app, Speech4Good, which helps stutterers improve speech.
- Eric and Matt Lowe of Emerson College are the co-founders of Quiyk, a company that makes athletic apparel for Quidditch, a fictional sport from the Harry Potter novels.

"When you create more small businesses, you create small entrepreneurship. Out of that comes self-determination and employment."

JESSE JACKSON

"Pessimism is an excuse for not trying and a guarantee to a personal failure."

BILL CLINTON

# Quiz

## Online Resources and Interviewing

1. Personal branding involves
   a. using brand name products.
   b. avoiding name brand products to save money.
   c. using social media to market yourself.

2. One step in managing your online presence is to
   a. limit your use of online tools.
   b. remove inappropriate content.
   c. turn off all privacy controls.

3. At the present time, the most common social media used by employers to research job candidates are
   a. Twitter and Facebook
   b. Tumblr and Instagram
   c. LinkedIn and Facebook

4. The first step in the interview process is
   a. to research information about the company and the job.
   b. ask the interviewer about salary and vacation time.
   c. prepare casual and comfortable clothes.

5. The informational interview is
   a. a good way to find career information and build your network.
   b. a good way to ask for a job.
   c. controlled by the employer.

**How did you do on the quiz? Check your answers: 1. c, 2. b, 3. c, 4. a, 5. a**

# Taking Action

The most important and challenging part of your job search is taking action. Realize that finding a job requires time management and hard work, but it will all pay off when you find a good job. Also realize that you will do many job searches over a lifetime, so keep your resume tuned up, do the best at your current job so that you can get good references, and maintain your professional network.

There will be times when you do not receive a response to a job application, do not get an interview, or do not get the job you consider to be your dream job. It is essential to realize that these are all part of the job search process and to maintain a positive attitude.

Here is a checklist for beginning your job search action plan:

_____ Find out what resources your college Career Services office provides.

_____ Attend job fairs and career conferences.

_____ Assess your skills (multiple intelligences), interests, and personal strengths.

© CURIOSO.PHOTOGRAPHY/SHUTTERSTOCK.COM

_____ Complete career research on your areas of interest. What are the job activities, skills required, and career outlook?

_____ Investigate opportunities for volunteering and internships.

_____ Identify your goals. Where do you want to be in six months? A year? Five years?

_____ Create your personal brand based on your personal strengths and how they match the job market, including potential job titles.

_____ Set up a Facebook and LinkedIn account if you have not already done so. If you have an existing account check to make sure it is appropriate for a prospective employer to view.

_____ Complete your resume and cover letter.

_____ Do some informational interviews.

_____ Compile reference letters.

_____ Practice interview questions.

_____ Prepare your interview clothes.

_____ Search online career databases for current job openings.

_____ Write thank you letters to anyone helping you in your search.

_____ Use time management. Make a To Do list for each day and set goals for the week and month.

_____ Organize a job search system to keep track of resumes sent, employers contacted, and any other actions taken on your job search. Keep a simple diary that includes these items.

_____ Keep a positive attitude. Stay physically, emotionally, and mentally healthy during your job search.

As you are conducting your job search, ask these questions to evaluate how you are doing:

- What is working well? What is not working?
- How can I improve?
- What resources are available? Where can I go or who can I ask for help?
- How can I stay motivated?

> "Many of life's failures are people who do not realize how close they were to success when they gave up."
> THOMAS EDISON

# Keys to Success
## Create Your Future

We are responsible for what happens in our lives. We make decisions and choices that create the future. Our behavior leads to success or failure. Too often we believe that we are victims of circumstance. When looking at our lives, we often look for others to blame for how our life is going:

- My grandparents did it to me. I inherited these genes.
- My parents did it to me. My childhood experiences shaped who I am.
- My teacher did it to me. He gave me a poor grade.
- My boss did it to me. She gave me a poor evaluation.
- The government did it to me. All my money goes to taxes.
- Society did it to me. I have no opportunity.

These factors are powerful influences in our lives, but we are still left with choices. Concentration camp survivor Viktor Frankl wrote a book, *Man's Search for Meaning*, in which he describes his experiences and how he survived his ordeal. His parents, brother, and wife died in the camps. He suffered starvation and torture. Through all of his sufferings and imprisonment, he still maintained that he was a free man because he could make choices.

*We who lived in concentration camps can remember the men who walked through the huts comforting others, giving away their last piece of bread. They may have been few in number, but they offer sufficient proof that everything can be taken from a man but one thing: the last of the human freedoms—to choose one's attitude in any given set of circumstances, to choose one's own way.*

*. . . Fundamentally, therefore, any man can, even under such circumstances, decide what shall become of him— mentally and spiritually. He may retain his human dignity even in a concentration camp.*[6]

Viktor Frankl could not choose his circumstances at that time, but he did choose his attitude. He decided how he would respond to the situation. He realized that he still had the freedom to make choices. He used his memory and imagination to exercise his freedom. When times were the most difficult, he would imagine that he was in the classroom lecturing to his students about psychology. He eventually did get out of the concentration camp and became a famous psychiatrist.

Hopefully none of you will ever have to experience the circumstances faced by Viktor Frankl, but we all face challenging situations. It is empowering to think that our behavior is more a function of our decisions rather than our circumstances. It is not productive to look around and find someone to blame for your problems. Psychologist Abraham Maslow says that instead of blaming we should see how we can make the best of the situation.

*One can spend a lifetime assigning blame, finding a cause, "out there" for all the troubles that exist. Contrast this with the responsible attitude of confronting the situation, bad or good, and instead of asking, "What caused the trouble? Who was to blame?", asking, "How can I handle the present situation to make the best of it?"*[7]

Author Stephen Covey suggests that we look at the word responsibility as "response-ability."[8] It is the ability to choose responses and make decisions about the future. When you are dealing with a problem, it is useful to ask yourself what decisions you made that led to the problem. How did you create the situation? If you created the problem, you can create a solution.

At times, you may ask, "How did I create this?", and find that the answer is that you did not create the situation. We certainly do not create earthquakes or hurricanes, for example. But we do create or at least contribute to many of the things that happen to us. Even if you did not create your circumstances, you can create your reaction to the situation. In the case of an earthquake, you can decide to panic or find the best course of action at the moment.

Stephen Covey believes that we can use our resourcefulness and initiative in dealing with most problems. When his children were growing up and they asked him how to solve a certain problem, he would say, "Use your R and I!". He meant resourcefulness and initiative. He notes that adults can use this R and I to get a good job.

> *But the people who end up with the good jobs are the proactive ones who are solutions to problems, not problems themselves, who seize the initiative to do whatever is necessary, consistent with correct principles, to get the job done.*[9]

Use your resourcefulness and initiative to create the future that you want.

## Journal Entry

How can you create the future you want for yourself?

**5**

## JOURNAL ENTRIES
## UPDATED JOB SEARCH STRATEGIES

Go to http://www.collegesuccess1.com/JournalEntries.htm for Word files of the Journal Entries.

## SUCCESS
## over the Internet

**Visit the *College Success Website* at http://www.collegesuccess1.com/**

The *College Success Website* is continually updated with new topics and links to the material presented in this chapter. Topics include:

- Information about internships and volunteering
- Resume templates
- Sample resumes and cover letters
- Examples of personal brands
- Information on interviewing
- Tips for starting your own business

Contact your instructor if you have any problems in accessing the *College Success Website*.

# Notes

1.  Kelsey Lucier, "Consider Pros and Cons of Working in College," www.usnews .com, September 13, 2012.

2.  Scott Kirsner, "Some Graduates Diving Right into Business," www. bostonglobe.com, April 28, 2013.

3.  Felicia Joy, "College Entrepreneurs: 25 Business Ideas That Students Can Launch for $200 or Less," feliciajoyonline.wordpress.com, August 6, 2011.

4.  Courtney Rubin, "Create Your Own College Job," www.usnews.com, September 27, 2012.

5.  Mariana Simoes and Max Nisen, "16 Great Startups College Students are Working on Right Now," www.businessinsider.com, February 11, 2013.

6.  Viktor Frankl, *Man's Search for Meaning* (New York: Pocket Books, 1963), 104–105.

7.  Quoted in Rob Gilbert, ed., *Bits and Pieces*, November 4, 1999.

8.  Stephen Covey, The *7 Habits of Highly Effective People* (New York: Simon and Schuster, 1989), 71.

9.  Ibid., 75.

# SAMPLE COVER LETTER

Sara Student
222 College Avenue
San Diego, CA 92019
(619) 123-4567

June 20, 2021

Mr. John Smith
Director of Human Resources
Future Technology Company
111 Technology Way
La Jolla, CA 92111

Dear Mr. Smith:

At our college job fair last week, I enjoyed speaking with you about some new engineering jobs available at Future Technology Company. As you suggested, I am sending my resume. I am interested in your opening for an electrical engineer. Is there anything else I need to do to apply for this position?

While at UCSD, I gained experience in laboratory projects, writing scientific reports, and preparing technical presentations. Some engineering projects that I completed relate to work done at your company:

- Constructed a programmable robot with motor and sensors

- Worked with a group of students on the design of a satellite communications system

- Completed lab projects on innovative fiber-optic fabrication techniques

- Proposed a design for a prosthetic device to help the visually impaired

For my senior design project, I used my knowledge of digital signal processing and systems integration to design and construct a voice modulator. This project involved applying theory to hardware and understanding information processing as well as the relation of a computer to its controlled devices.

I am excited about the possibility of continuing work in this field and would enjoy the opportunity to discuss my qualifications in more detail. I am available for an interview at your convenience. I look forward to hearing from you.

Sincerely,

Sara Student

Encl.: Resume

# SAMPLE RESUME FOR A RECENT COLLEGE GRADUATE

**Sara Student**
222 College Avenue; San Diego, CA 92019
(619) 123-4567
saraengineer@aol.com

OBJECTIVE

Electrical Engineer

HIGHLIGHTS

Recent degree in Electrical Engineering
Specialized coursework in electromagnetism, photonics and lasers, biomedical imaging devices, and experimental techniques

EDUCATION

B.S., Electrical Engineering, University of California, San Diego, CA, 2021
A.S. with Honors, Cuyamaca College, El Cajon, CA, 2018

KEY RELATED COURSES
- **Circuits and systems:** solving network equations, Laplace transforms, practical robotics development
- **Electromagnetism:** Maxwell's equations, wave guides and transmission, electromagnetic properties of circuits and materials
- **Experimental techniques:** built and programmed a voice processor; studied transducers, computer architecture, and interfacing; applied integrated construction techniques
- **Photonics and lasers:** laser stability and design, holography, optical information processing, pattern recognition, electro-optic modulation, fiber optics
- **Biomedical imaging devices:** microscopy, x-rays, and neural imaging; designed an optical prosthesis
- **Quantum physics:** uncertainty principle, wave equation and spin, particle models, scattering theory and radiation

SKILLS

**Computer Skills:** PSpice, Matlab, Java, DSP, Assembly Language, Unix, Windows, Microsoft Word, Excel, and PowerPoint
**Technical Skills:** Microprocessors, circuits, optical components, oscilloscope, function generator, photovoltaics, signal processing, typing, SQUID testing
**Personal Skills:** Leadership, good people skills, organized, responsible, creative, motivated, hardworking, good writing skills

EMPLOYMENT  Intern, Quantum Design, La Jolla, CA, Summer 2019
Computer Lab Assistant, UCSD, La Jolla, CA, 2019–2020
Teacher's Aide, Cuyamaca College, El Cajon, CA, 2016–2018
Volunteer, Habitat for Humanity, Tijuana, Mexico, 2015–2016

INTERESTS  Optics, computing, programming, physics, electronic music, sampling, marine biology, and scuba diving

ACHIEVEMENTS  Advanced Placement Scholar
Dean's List, Phi Theta Kappa Honor Society
Provost's Honors List

# RESUME WORKSHEET FOR YOUR IDEAL CAREER

Use this worksheet to prepare a resume similar to the sample on the previous page. Assume that you have graduated from college and are applying for your ideal career.

1. What is the specific job title of your ideal job?

2. What are two or three qualifications you possess that would especially qualify you for this job? These qualifications can be listed under Highlights on your resume.

3. List your degree or degrees, major, and dates of completion.

4. List five courses you will take to prepare for your ideal career. For each course, list some key components that would catch the interest of your potential employer. Use a college catalog to complete this section.

5. List the skills you would need in each of these areas.

Computer skills:

Technical or other job-related skills:

Personal skills related to your job objective:

6. List employment that would prepare you for your ideal job. Consider internships or part-time employment.

7. What are your interests?

8. What special achievements or awards do you have?

# INTERVIEW WORKSHEET

Answer the following questions to prepare for the interview for your ideal job. If you do not know what your ideal job is, pretend that you are interviewing for any professional job. You may want to practice these questions with a classmate.

1. What can you tell us about yourself?

2. Why are you leaving your present job?

3. What are your strengths and weaknesses?

4. Tell us about a difficulty or problem that you solved on the job.

5. Tell us about one of your achievements on the job.

6. What do you like best about your work? What do you like least?

7. Are there any questions that you would like to ask?

# Career Satisfaction

# 7

## OBJECTIVES

Read to answer these key questions:

- How can I find meaning and passion in my work?

- How important is money for my job satisfaction?

- What are some predictors of job satisfaction?

- How can I be successful in my job?

- What are my lifetime goals?

- How do my thoughts create my success?

Too often people think of work as something unpleasant, and hate Monday mornings. They live for the weekends. Throughout history, work was something that people dreamed of escaping.

> Even Cinderella was locked in a contract doing long hours of menial low paid work and left dreaming of escape. Meanwhile Jack gladly exchanged the hard work of the farm for a few magic beans and a chance encounter with a beanstalk. Upon his return, Jack (like Cinderella) had no need to work and lived happily ever after. The giant he slayed was work. The dream of escaping this ogre is common to us all.[1]

Is work the problem? A job is often what we make of it. Lots of people happily run a marathon, grow plants, create art, and write for fun. Many find personal meaning in work, and it becomes part of our identity. Our attitude toward work is largely determined by our thinking about it. Loving your job is a little like climbing a mountain. It takes some effort, but the results are satisfying. Working Monday through Friday makes the weekend something to anticipate. It is ironic that we must work Monday through Friday to feel happy about not working over the weekend.

It is unrealistic to expect that you will enjoy every day at work or like all your work, but it is good to enjoy your work at least most of the time. In this chapter, we examine the components of career satisfaction so that you can enjoy the work that you do. It is not good to hate Mondays.

© BABAYUKA/SHUTTERSTOCK.COM

## Find Your Passion

It is often recommended that finding your passion can make work more satisfying. Finding your passion, however, is not so easy. Some are lucky to find a passion that matches their lifestyle, values, and skills. Many people find it difficult to identify their passion. Still others find a job and then develop a passion for it as their skills and success increase. As an example, Steve Jobs,

Apple cofounder, was an advocate of following your passion. In his youth, he was passionate about Zen Buddhism, Western history, and dance. He started working in technology to make money. It was only when he became successful in technology that he became passionate about it. It is interesting to consider the possibility that passion increases when we become good at something and experience success in it.[2]

It is also possible that your passion may limit your opportunities. If you are passionate about becoming a nurse, but cannot meet the math and science requirements, you may become frustrated and not consider other equally satisfying health careers. Many students are passionate about careers in sports, arts, or music, however, there are very limited career opportunities in these fields. Because of limited opportunities, you may have to use some creative job search strategies, invent your own career, or find your passion in careers that have more opportunities. Remember that you can further develop passion by improving your skills and achieving success in your work.

It is important to note that interests are not static and that they change over a lifetime. Begin your search for passion by focusing on what helps others. Start with how you can make a valuable contribution to the world and then it is easier to develop a passion for it.

The best way to find your passion is to look at the world and find out what problems need solving, select those that interest you, and work to improve your skills. In this way, you can find more satisfying job opportunities.

# Finding Meaning in Your Work

Meaningful work is connected to job satisfaction, overall personal well-being, and happiness. How we think about our jobs creates meaning. There is a famous story about three bricklayers. When asked, "What are you doing?" the first worker replies that he is putting one brick on top of another. This worker has a job. The second replies that he is making a salary. This worker has a career. The third replies that he is building a cathedral. He views his work as personally meaningful. This worker has a calling. Meaning depends on how you think about your job. You can find meaning in a variety of ways:

Does my job

- Provide for my basic needs?
- Allow me to support my family?
- Give me the opportunity to pursue my favorite recreational activities when I am not working?
- Help me to improve my skills and be the best I can be?
- Allow me to take pride in my work?
- Contribute to the greater good?
- Utilize my unique skills and talents?
- Provide recognition, respect, and praise for a job well done?
- Provide constructive feedback for improvement?

One of the ways of finding meaning in work is through a process called "job crafting," which is changing your job to match your strengths, interests, and values. Here are the steps in job crafting[3]:

1. Look at the tasks you are doing on the job, decide which tasks you like best, and spend more time on these tasks.
2. Volunteer for additional tasks you might enjoy.
3. Master your current role and then find creative ways to expand it so that it matches your personal strengths.
4. Learn new skills that can make you more productive on the job.
5. Spend more time with people that you like on the job.
6. Change the way you think about your job and make the most of the job you have. Think about how it improves the well-being of others, contributes to the goals of the business, or gets the job done. As an example, zookeepers find meaning in cleaning animal cages because they are helping animals and preserving species.

**Journal Entry**

Write five sentences about finding passion and meaning in your career.

## Money and Job Satisfaction

Many students are motivated to attend college to have financial security while others focus more finding meaningful work that is more important than potential income. Both options are explored in the following sections.

# Money Is Important

One of the strongest motivators for attending college is to be financially secure. This is especially true for first-generation college students and for those who live in areas where the cost of living is high. We have noted in previous chapters that education improves income as well as employment opportunities.

If high income is important to you, begin by thinking about your attitude toward math. Are you good at math or can you develop an interest in it? Math is required for high-paying jobs in engineering, science, technology, computer science, business, economics, accounting, finance, and health occupations. These occupations have high salaries and an excellent career outlook.

It is interesting to think about your interests and how they can change and develop over a lifetime. While matching your interests to a career is important for your happiness and satisfaction, interests can change over a lifetime and are often dependent on personal experiences. For example, if you know someone who is an engineer, and you can do an engineering internship, you may develop an interest in this field. If you have never had any experiences with engineering, it is difficult to know if you could be interested in it. An important part of career exploration is engaging in experiences that let you know about all career options, including internships, volunteering, career research, and informational interviewing with people in different occupations.

Your experiences are also a good way to find out if a career is right for you. For example, you may be interested in teaching. Spending time volunteering in a classroom can give you a realistic picture of this occupation to determine if it matches your personal strengths and interests. It is best to have these experiences early in your education so that you do not spend time on a major and then find out that you do not like the occupation.

Attaining wealth is also dependent both on your attitude and how you manage your money. Warren Buffet, one of the richest men on earth, provides these tips for attaining wealth:[4,5]

© KRISTA KENNELL/SHUTTERSTOCK.COM

- **Believe in being rich.** To be rich, you must believe that one day you will be rich and start taking the steps to achieve your goal. Buffet states that, "I always knew I would be rich. I don't think I ever doubted it for a second."
- **Start saving at a young age.** It is important to begin saving money at a young age so that you get in the habit of saving money. At the age of 15, Warren Buffet began saving money from his job delivering newspapers and selling magazine subscriptions. He used his savings to invest in a profit-sharing agreement with a farmer.
- **Reinvest your profits.** When in high school, Buffet invested in pin ball machines. He used all his profits to purchase additional machines. He eventually sold this business for a profit.
- **Graduate college early.** You can save money by finishing college early. You not only save the costs of college, but you have more time to earn money in your career.
- **Bounce back from rejection.** Buffet was turned down for his application to Harvard Business School. Buffet states, "Turned down? Who cares, keep going, it happens all the time." He was accepted at Columbia. This attitude relates to the growth mindset in that setbacks are viewed as opportunities.
- **Communicate in person.** If you are trying to accomplish your goals, an email or phone call may not work. In-person communication is the most powerful.
- **Invest in "you" before anything else.** Buffet suggests, "Find your passion, invest in yourself through gaining wisdom and knowledge, and never, ever, stop learning."

- **Break bad habits early.** The worst habit is using credit cards to purchase items you cannot afford.
- **Find your strengths.** It is important to be aware of your strengths and match them to your career. You can always work on improving your strengths to increase opportunities.
- **Do what you love.** You cannot be happy spending your life in misery.
- **Don't pass up good opportunities.** Realize that these good opportunities may require hard work and can make you feel uncomfortable, but take advantage of them.
- **Protect your clock.** Learn as much about time management as you can. Become a master of your time.
- **Be kind.** Buffet suggest that we learn kindness, learn it early, and use it often.

The real value of money is that it can buy freedom and security. With more money, you have more time to enjoy your life and the freedom to do what you want. You can further your education or spend time traveling. You can feel good about contributing to others.

## Money Is Not So Important

Does more money lead to job satisfaction? Some interesting research shows that money does makes you happier, but only a little. Beyond a salary of $50,000–$75,000 a year, income has little relationship to daily happiness. Note that the average college graduate earns about $77,000 a year, which fits into this happiness range.[6] We can all think of famous movie stars, sports celebrities, and powerful business people who have high incomes and are not happy in life. Once you have met your basic needs, increased income does not make you much happier.

You may be happy about getting a raise, but you quickly get used to it and you become just about as happy as you were before the raise. Research has shown that lottery winners receive a short-term boost in happiness, but return to their previous level of happiness in a short time. This short-lived happiness is due to the process of hedonistic adaptation.[7] Hedonistic adaptation means that as you acquire more material possessions, you easily get used to them, and then want something better. Once you have the newest model TV, it is no longer important, and you start thinking about a bigger and better one. The resulting increased debt can cause even greater unhappiness. To avoid hedonistic adaptation, it is helpful to separate what you need from what you want.

A king was going to his palace after his rounds in the city when he met a beggar. He asked the beggar, "What would you like?" the beggar laughed and said, "You are asking me as though you can fulfill my desire!" The king was offended. He said, "Of course I can fulfill your desire. What is it? Just tell me." And the beggar said, "Think twice before you promise anything."

"I will fulfill anything you ask. I am a powerful king. What can you possibly desire that I cannot give to you?" The beggar said, "It is a very simple desire. You see this begging bowl? Can you fill it with something?" The king said, "Of course!" He called his vizier and told him, "Fill this man's begging bowl with money." The vizier went and got some money and poured it into the bowl, and it disappeared. And he poured more and more, and the moment he would pour it, it would disappear. And the begging bowl remained always empty.

The whole palace gathered. By and by the rumor went throughout the city, and a huge crowd gathered. The prestige of the king was at stake. He said to his vizier, "If the whole kingdom is lost, I am ready to lose it, but I cannot be defeated by this beggar." Diamonds and pearls and emeralds, his treasures becoming empty. The begging bowl seemed to be bottomless. Everything that was put into it immediately disappeared, went out of existence.

Finally, it was evening, and the people were standing there in utter silence. The king dropped at the feet of the beggar and admitted his defeat. He said, "Just tell me one thing. You are victorious- but before you leave, just fulfill my curiosity. What is the begging bowl made of?"

The beggar laughed and said, "There is no secret. It is simply made of human desire."[8]

Understanding human desire and hedonistic adaptation can change your attitude toward money and reevaluate its importance in career satisfaction. Money alone cannot buy happiness or satisfaction.

## Journal Entry

Write five sentences about income and your job satisfaction.

**2**

## Predictors of Job Satisfaction

Being unsatisfied with your job has several negative consequences. It can lead to lower productivity on the job, poor job performance, increased job stress, and high turnover rates. It can result in lower employee morale and less company loyalty. Ultimately and most importantly, it leads to unhappiness in the workplace. How can you be more satisfied with your job?

**Researchers have discovered the factors that lead to job satisfaction.** Many of these factors are within our control. Positive psychologist Martin Seligman has identified several elements that contribute to well-being[9]:

- Positive emotion, including happiness and life satisfaction
- Engagement
- Relationships
- Meaning
- Achievement

Other psychologists have identified additional factors contributing to well-being[10]:

- Competence: Experiencing control and mastery
- Relatedness: Connecting with others
- Autonomy: Having choice and control

How does this research relate to job satisfaction?

**Meeting your basic needs** is an important component of satisfying careers. Basic needs include working hours, job security, time required for traveling to work, and fair pay. Working reasonable hours that provide for a work and life balance is part of your basic needs. Working long hours that interfere with your personal and family life is stressful and less satisfying. Having job security provides the confidence that you will be able to meet your basic needs. Having a long commute to work limits productivity and decreases satisfaction. People are most dissatisfied with commutes of over 60 minutes.[11] It is important that the pay you receive is comparable to other people doing the same type of work.

**Satisfying jobs have some stress.** We often think of a dream job as one that has less stress. However, an undemanding job can be boring. Workers are more highly motivated when there are high demands that are achievable.

Those who experience job satisfaction have a growth mindset and view problems as opportunities in which stress provides the motivation to achieve positive results. Accomplishing difficult tasks provides a sense of achievement. People can deal with stress, and be motivated by it, if they have the control and autonomy to complete the job along with a supportive work environment.

**Work that helps others** is one of the best predictors of job satisfaction. Helping others increases meaning and purpose in life, one of the factors contributing to well-being.

**Engaging work** is more satisfying. Surveys of job satisfaction show that engaging, challenging, and interesting work is even more important than pay or status. Engaging work includes variety, clearly defined tasks, a sense of completion, autonomy, feedback on performance, and a sense of contribution. You are engaged in your work when you are focused and productive.

**Being good at your job** contributes to satisfaction because it contributes to a sense of achievement. When you are good at your job, you can take on more meaningful and interesting assignments, as well as earn a fair salary. Stress is lowered when you have the skills to do your job along with the belief that you can do the job well.

**Working with people you like** leads to increased job satisfaction. A disagreeable person can ruin a dream job, while working with a friend can make even a boring or tedious job fun. Having satisfying personal relationships are an important part of enjoying your job. This includes being able to get help and advice from others on the job as well as making friends with at least some of the people with whom you work.

In summary, to find your dream job, look for work that

- Meets your basic needs for income and working conditions
- Matches your skills
- Is engaging and interesting
- Helps others
- Has good working conditions such as supportive colleagues, fair pay, and work that helps you to maintain a balance in work and life
- Matches your personal values

**Research has shown what makes people happy at work.** Here are some of the findings about happiness at work:[12]

- **Autonomy** is having control over your work. You have more autonomy when you can manage your own time, make decisions, and have some control over your work.
- **Being self-employed** provides workers more autonomy and happiness, although those who are self-employed tend to work longer hours. Those who are self-employed have more control over their destiny, and take responsibility for their own success. It is interesting that autonomy is

Those only are happy who have their minds fixed on some object other than their own happiness; on the happiness of others, on the improvement of mankind, even on some art or pursuit, followed not as a means, but as itself an ideal end. Aiming thus at something else, they find happiness by the way.

-JOHN STUART MILL

Set your heart on doing good. Do it over and over again and you will be filled with joy.

-BUDDHA

A man's true wealth is the good he does in this world.

-MUHAMMAD

Every man must decide whether he will walk in the light of creative altruism or in the darkness of destructive selfishness.

-MARTIN LUTHER KING, JR.

often valued as more important than income for many people. People with high income and less autonomy are less happy than those with lower pay and more autonomy.

- **Mastery** is an important component of happiness on the job. Being able to use your skills and improve them adds satisfaction and happiness. Mastery is related to "flow activities" in which you feel totally involved in what you are doing without noticing the passage of time.
- **Variety** is another component of happiness. Having variety creates interest.
- **Getting positive feedback about your work** is a great motivator and adds to happiness on the job. Good managers provide positive and useful feedback to employees.
- **Being able to finish the job is important.** Workers who can start a project and work through to completion are happier than those doing just part of a job.
- **Having friends at work** adds to the enjoyment of working.
- **Having a work environment that allows you to focus** on the work adds to happiness. Frequent interruptions can be stressful.
- **Living close to work** is another key job satisfier.
- **Working to contribute to the greater good** increases happiness.
- **Pursuing meaningful goals throughout life** by continuing to work leads to greater happiness and longevity.

## Journal
### Entry

| Make a list of five items important for satisfaction in your career. | **3** |

# How to Be Successful in Your Job

Once you have found that dream job, how can you be successful in your new career? Develop your job skills, improve your emotional intelligence, learn good communication skills, and follow some general tips for success.

© BRASIL CREATIVO/SHUTTERSTOCK.COM

## Essential Work Skills for 2020 and Beyond

Because of rapid changes in technology and society, it is important to keep your skills up to date. Current research has identified the top skills needed for career success.[13]

- **Creativity.** Brainstorm many solutions to problems and then select the best one.
- **Complex problem solving.** This involves analytical and logical thinking.
- **Dealing with unpredictable change.** Realize that the world is changing quickly, and change is necessary.
- **Emotional intelligence.** This is defined as the ability to recognize, control, and evaluate your own emotions while realizing how they affect people around you.
- **Understanding other departments.** Take some time to get to know people from other departments and understand their contribution to the whole organization.
- **People management.** Develop skills in collaboration, teamwork, and leadership. An essential component to people management is developing empathy, which is the ability to understand and share the feelings of others.
- **Using new media and communication.** Keep up with the new media tools used in collaboration and communication.
- **Cultural cross fluency.** Awareness and appreciation of other cultures improves communication and collaboration along with the ability to participate in the global economy.
- **Decision making skills.** This skill is important for leadership and effective management.
- **Negotiation skills.** These skills are important in reaching common ground and avoiding confrontation.

## Emotional Intelligence and Career Success

Those with a high level of emotional intelligence are more likely to be successful on the job. In review, emotional intelligence is defined as the ability to recognize, control, and evaluate your own emotions while realizing how they affect people around you. Emotional intelligence is related to interpersonal and intrapersonal intelligences, as described in Chapter 4. Here is a summary of emotional intelligence and how it is related to career success. People with emotional intelligence

- Have a high level of self-awareness and understand their emotions, strengths, weaknesses and motivation. They have a direction in life and understand their goals and values.
- Can manage their emotions so that these emotions do not control their words and actions. We all have bad moods, but don't need to let emotions create problems on the job.

- Show empathy for others. Showing empathy means understanding the needs and emotions of others and considering their feelings when communicating, taking action, or making decisions.
- Have good social skills. Having social skills involves being friendly as well as finding common ground with a variety of people even though you may disagree with them. People with social skills are good team players and can bring diverse people together to accomplish the goals of the workplace.

## Communication for Career Success

Effective communication skills can increase your success on the job and improve your relationships with others who are important to you. Many colleges require public speaking and communication skills for graduation, and they are important for your success. Here are some key ideas.

**Personal communication style.** Your personality type has a major influence on communication. Review the communication section of your TruTalent Personality assessment to learn about your communication strengths and some areas for improvement.

**Friendliness.** Being honest and kind can help to build trust and friendships on the job. Asking others how they are doing, smiling, and offering praise for a job well done helps to improve relationships with co-workers and managers.

**Confidence.** Project confidence by maintaining eye contact, using good posture, and preparing ahead so that you can express your ideas thoughtfully.

**Feedback.** Providing and accepting feedback is an important skill in improving job performance. Listen carefully during critical feedback. When giving feedback to others remember that the best feedback answers questions, provides solutions, and offers suggestions for improvement.

**Empathy.** Understanding the feelings, ideas, and goals of others can help you to improve communication with them. Empathy involves understanding other people's emotions and selecting an appropriate response. If someone is angry or frustrated, empathy can help you to acknowledge and diffuse the emotion. If someone is feeling happy or enthusiastic, show understanding and help celebrate their success.

**Respect.** Allowing others to speak without interruption shows respect. Respect also means staying on topic, asking good questions, and responding to questions.

**Responsiveness.** It is important to return emails and phone calls quickly. People who communicate quickly are viewed as more effective.

**Be a good listener.** The first step to effective communication is learning to be a good listener. It is important to listen first to gain an understanding of the other person before you speak. Often, people are thinking about what they are going to say next rather than listening to others. This habit leads to lack of understanding. Listening is hard work, requiring effort, attention, and striving to understand. Those with good listening skills are held in high regard by their co-workers because of the respect they pay to others around them. Listening skills are especially important in developing leadership skills.

**Ask questions.** You will need to ask questions to make sure you understand. Each person looks at the world in a different way. The picture in your mind probably does not match the picture that others have. Increase understanding by asking questions. Asking questions also shows that you care.

**Feedback meaning.** This communication technique involves restating the speaker's ideas in your own works to check meaning. This is important because speakers often:

- say one thing and mean something else.
- say something but don't mean it, especially if emotions are involved.
- speak in a way that causes confusion.

Feeding back meaning has two important benefits. It helps speakers to clarify their thoughts and it helps listeners make sure that they have received the correct message. You can feedback meaning by:

- Restating what has been said.
  Statement: Please complete this project right away.
  Feedback: So, you are saying that this project is top priority, right?
- Asking for clarification.
  Statement: Complete this financial report for our next meeting.
  Feedback: This report is for the manager's meeting on Monday, right?
- Rewording the message to check for understanding.
  Statement: I need this project completed by Friday.
  Feedback: So, this project needs to be done by Friday. What parts do you want included and how would you like me to do it?

**Search for win-win solutions.** In a win-win approach, both parties work together to find a solution that meets everyone's needs. There is no loser. To reach a win-win solution, set aside competition and replace it with cooperation. This is often difficult to do because emotions are involved. It is important to put aside emotions to discuss the issue. This may mean waiting until both parties have had the opportunity to calm down. Strive to remain calm, especially in business relationships.

## Some Barriers to Effective Communication

We all want to communicate effectively and to get along with people we care about. We want to get along with our families, be a good parent, have friends at school, get along with the boss, and have good relationships with our co-workers on the job. Watch for these barriers to effective communication.

- **Criticizing**
  Making a negative evaluation of others by saying, "It's your fault," or "I told you so," causes anger, which gets in the way of communication.
- **Name-calling and Labeling**
  If you call someone a name or put a label on them, they will attack you rather than communicate with you in any meaningful way.

- **Giving Advice**
  Giving advice is often viewed as talking down to a person. They may resent both you and your advice.
- **Ordering or Commanding**
  If you order someone to do something, they are likely to sabotage your request.
- **Threatening**
  Trying to control by making threats causes resentment.
- **Moralizing**
  Preaching about what a person should or should not do doesn't work because it causes resentment.
- **Diverting**
  Changing the subject to talk about your own problems tells the person that you do not care about them.
- **Logical Arguing**
  Trying to use facts to convince without taking feelings into account is a barrier to communication. Present your facts and state your point of view, but respect the other person's feelings and different point of view.

## Some Tips for Career Success

Here are some tips to consider as you begin a new job:

- **Behave as if you are still being interviewed.**  Make a good impression from the first day. Show up every day and do a good job to prove to your employer that you deserved to be hired.
- **Help the manager get the job done.**  Understand what needs to be done and work to accomplish the goals of the organization. In this way, your value to the company will increase.
- **Clarify expectations.**  Find out what the priorities are and what is expected of you. Ask for feedback about your work and how you can do better if there are any problems.
- **Ask for help.**  Asking for help is much better than doing the job incorrectly. Asking for help is not a sign of weakness; it is a sign of strength.
- **Build good relationships with your coworkers.**  Be courteous, tactful, and friendly. Make an effort to get to know your coworkers. Build trust by getting the job done. Practice listening to and supporting your coworkers. Avoid gossip which can lead to personal problems on the job.
- **Be a team player.**  Most careers involve working with others to come up with creative ideas and get the job done. Be supportive of others on the team and recognize their contributions and achievements.
- **Learn something new.**  Realize that every new employee lacks the skills and experience of others who have been on the job for a while. Take advantage of opportunities to learn new skills.

- **Welcome constructive criticism.** Remember that suggestions can be an opportunity for improvement, and don't take them personally.
- **Have a positive attitude.** Thinking positively will help you get the job done and enjoy it more.
- **Keep a record of your accomplishments.** Save emails, positive feedback, and successful projects. They can be useful for performance reviews and promotions.
- **Remember to exercise.** Exercise can lower stress, improve your health, and enhance job performance. Find out how other employees exercise during or after the work-day and join in with them. You can make new friends in the process.
- **Dress for success.** Take a look at what successful employees wear and dress professionally. In most professional positions, it is wise to cover tattoos and remove visible body piercings.
- **Show up on time.** It shows respect for others at work.
- **Become familiar** with the new media and virtual communication tools increasingly used in business today.
- **Become aware** of your own culture and respect the cultural differences of others. Appreciating diversity leads to greater creativity and teamwork.
- **Minimize conflict** by striving to find common ground with others.

## Journal Entry

Write five intention statements about being successful on the job.

## What Are My Lifetime Goals?

Now that you have explored your personality, interests, intelligences, and values and thought about career satisfaction, it is a good time to think about some goals for the future. Setting goals helps you to establish what is important and provides direction for your life. Goals help you to focus your energy on what you want to accomplish. Goals are a promise to yourself to improve your life. Setting goals can help you turn your dreams into reality. Steven Scott in his book A Millionaire's Notebook, lays out five steps in this process:

1. Dream or visualize.
2. Convert the dream into goals.
3. Convert your goals into tasks.
4. Convert your task into steps.
5. Take your first step, and then the next.[14]

As you begin to think about your personal goals in life, make your goals specific and concrete. Rather than saying, "I want to be rich," make your goal something that you can break into specific steps. You might want to start learning about money management or begin a savings plan. Rather than setting a goal for happiness, think about what brings you happiness. If you want to live a long and healthy life, think about the health habits that will help you to accomplish your goal. You will need to break your goals down into specific tasks to be able to accomplish them.

© WINUI/SHUTTERSTOCK.COM

Here are some criteria for successful goal setting

1. **Is it specific and measurable?** Can it be counted or observed? The most common goal mentioned by students is happiness in life. What is happiness and how will you know when you have achieved it? Is happiness a career you enjoy, owning your own home, or a travel destination?
2. **Is it achievable?** Do I have the skills, abilities, and resources to accomplish this goal? If not, am I willing to spend the time to develop the skills, abilities, and resources needed to achieve this goal?
3. **Is it realistic?** Do I believe I can achieve it? Am I positive and optimistic about this goal?
4. **Is it timely?** When will you finish this goal? Set a date to accomplish your goal.
5. **What steps do you need to take to begin?** Are your willing to take action and start working on it?
6. **Do you want to do it?** Is this a goal you are choosing because it increases personal satisfaction rather than meeting a requirement or an expectation of someone else?
7. **Are you motivated to achieve it?** What are your rewards for achieving it?
8. **Does the goal match your values?** Is it important to you?

"A goal is a dream with a deadline."

NAPOLEON HILL

# A Goal or a Fantasy?

One of the best questions ever asked in my class was, "What is the difference between a goal and a fantasy?" As you look at your list of lifetime goals, are some of these items goals or fantasies? Think about this question as you read the following scenario:

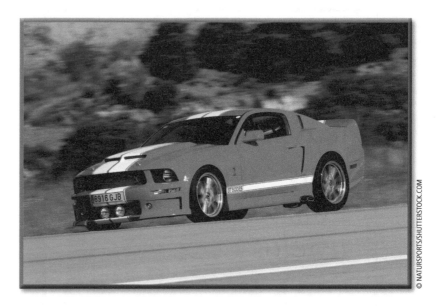

When Linda was a college student, she was walking through the parking lot and noticed a beautiful red sports car and decided that it would become a lifetime goal to own a similar car one day. However, with college expenses and her part-time job, it was not possible to buy the car. She would have to be content with the used car that her dad had given her so that she could drive to college. Years passed by, and Linda now has a good job, a home, and a family. She is reading a magazine and sees a picture of a similar red sports car. She cuts out this picture and tapes it to the refrigerator. After it has been on the refrigerator for several months, her children ask her why the picture is on the refrigerator. Linda replies, "I just like to dream about owning this car." One day as Linda is driving past a car dealership, she sees the red sports car on display and stops in for a test drive. To her surprise, she decides that she does not like driving the car. It doesn't fit her lifestyle either. She enjoys outdoor activities that would require a larger car. Buying a second car would be costly and reduce the amount of money that the family could spend on vacations. She decides that vacations are more important than owning the sports car. Linda goes home and removes the picture of the red sports car from the refrigerator.

There are many differences between a goal and a fantasy. A fantasy is a dream that may or may not become a reality. A goal is something that we actually plan to achieve. Sometimes we begin with a fantasy and later it becomes a goal. A fantasy can become a goal if steps are taken to achieve it.

In the preceding example, the sports car is a fantasy until Linda actually takes the car for a test drive. After driving the car, she decides that she really does not want it. The fantasy is sometimes better than the reality. Goals and fantasies change over a lifetime. We set goals, try them out, and change them as we grow and mature and find out what is most important in life. Knowing what we think is important, and what we value most, helps us make good decisions about lifetime goals.

What is the difference between a goal and a fantasy? A goal is something that requires action. Ask yourself if you are willing to take action on the goals you have set for yourself. Begin to take action by thinking about the steps needed to accomplish the goal. Then take the first step and continue. Change your goals if they are no longer important to you.

> "In life, as in football, you won't go far unless you know where the goalposts are."
>
> ARNOLD GLASGOW

## Use Priorities to Guide Your Actions

The **ABCs of time management** is a system of thinking about priorities. Priorities are what you think is important. An **A priority** is a task that relates to your lifetime goal. For example, if my goal is to earn a college degree, studying becomes an A priority. This activity would become one of the most important tasks that I could accomplish today. If my goal were to be healthy, an A priority would be to exercise and plan a healthy diet. If my goal is to have a good family life, an A priority would be to spend time with family members. Knowing about your lifetime goals and spending time on those items that are most important to you will help you to accomplish the goals that you have set for yourself. If you do not spend time on your goals, you may want to look at them again and decide which ones are fantasies that you do not really value or want to accomplish.

A **B priority** is an activity that you have to do but is not directly related to your lifetime goal. Examples of B priorities might be getting out of bed, taking a shower, buying groceries, paying bills, or getting gas for the car. These activities are less important but still are necessary for survival. If I do not put gas in the car, I cannot even get to school or work. If I do not pay the bills, I will soon have financial difficulties. While we often cannot postpone these activities in order to accomplish lifetime goals, we can learn efficient time management techniques to accomplish these tasks quickly.

A **C priority** is something that I can postpone until tomorrow with no harmful effect. For example, I could wait until tomorrow or another day to wash my car, do the laundry, buy groceries, or organize my desk. As these items are postponed, however, they can move up the list to a B priority. If I cannot see out of my car window or have no clean clothes to wear, it is time to move these tasks up on my list of priorities.

Have you ever been a victim of "**C fever**"? This is an illness in which we do the C activities first and do not get around to doing the A activities that are connected to lifetime goals. Tasks required to accomplish lifetime goals are often ones that are more difficult, challenge our abilities and take some time to accomplish. These tasks are often more difficult than the B or C activities. The C activities can fill our time and exhaust the energy we need to accomplish the A activities. An example of C fever is the student who cleans the desk or organizes the DVD collection instead of studying. C fever is doing the endless tasks that keep us from accomplishing goals that are really important to us. Why do we fall victim to C fever? C activities are often easy to do and give us a sense of accomplishment. We can see immediate progress without too much effort. I can wash my car and get a sense of accomplishment and satisfaction in my shiny clean car. The task is easy and does not challenge my intellectual capabilities.

# Activity

## Setting Priorities

To see how the ABCs of time management work, read the profile of Justin, a typical college student, below.

Justin is a 19-year-old college student who plans to major in physical therapy. He is athletic and values his good health. He cares about people and likes helping others. He has a part-time job working as an assistant in the gym, where he monitors proper use of the weight-lifting machines. Justin is also a member of the soccer team and practices with the team every afternoon.

Here is a list of activities that Justin would like to do today. Label each task as follows:

A if it relates to the Justin's lifetime goals

B if it is something necessary to do

C if it is something which could be done tomorrow or later

_____ Get up, shower, get dressed.

_____ Eat breakfast.

_____ Go to work.

_____ Go to class.

_____ Visit with friends between classes.

_____ Put gas in the car.

_____ Go shopping for new gym shoes.

_____ Attend soccer practice.

_____ Do weight-lifting exercises.

_____ Study for biology test that is tomorrow.

_____ Meet friends for pizza at lunch.

_____ Call girlfriend.

_____ Eat dinner.

_____ Unpack gear from weekend camping trip.

_____ Watch football game on TV.

_____ Play video games.

_____ Do math homework.

While Justin is the only one who can decide how to spend his time, he can take some steps toward accomplishing his lifetime goal of being healthy by eating properly, exercising, and going to soccer practice. He can become a physical therapist by studying for the biology test and doing his math homework. He can gain valuable experience related to physical therapy by working in the gym. He cares about people and likes to maintain good relationships with others. Any tasks related to these goals are high-priority A activities.

What other activities are necessary B activities? He certainly needs to get up, shower, get dressed, and put gas in the car if he plans to go somewhere. What are the C activities that could be postponed until tomorrow or later? Again Justin needs to decide. Maybe he could postpone shopping for gym shoes until the weekend. He would have to decide how much time to spend visiting with friends, watching TV, or playing video games. Since he likes these activities, he could use them as rewards for studying for the biology test and doing his math homework.

## Journal Entry

Using one of the most important goals you have identified for yourself, list some steps needed to accomplish it. What is the first step? Are you willing to begin taking these steps? Make a statement about your highest priority.

**5**

# Some Positive Thoughts for the Future

This course has provided you with the opportunity to increase self-understanding by learning about your personality type, intelligences, interests, values, and job skills. Use this knowledge to build your confidence and think positively about yourself. This knowledge is powerful because it will help you to make good decisions about your future based on your personal strengths and values. It is also important to understand the world of work and how you can best use your unique strengths, interests, and values to find a satisfying career. Take advantage of new technology to find your dream job based on what you find personally satisfying. Set some goals for the future

# Quiz

## Career Satisfaction

and begin to take action on them. Lastly, may you learn to enjoy your Mondays!

1.  Our attitude toward work is largely determined by
    a.  The type of work involved.
    b.  Our thinking about it.
    c.  The pay received.

2.  Passion increases with

a.  Skill improvement and achieving success.
b.  Multiple intelligences.
c.  Emotional intelligence.

3.  It is suggested that you can increase job satisfaction by
    a.  Asking for a raise.
    b.  Asking for a promotion.
    c.  Job crafting.

4.  Career interests are dependent on

    **a.** Heredity.
    **b.** Personal experiences with the career.
    **c.** The level of income.

**5.** According to researchers, the best predictor of career satisfaction is

    **a.** Money.
    **b.** Work that helps others or contributes to the common good.
    **c.** Work that leaves time for recreation.

**6.** Warren Buffet says that one of the most important factors in attaining wealth is

    **a.** Selecting the highest paying careers.
    **b.** Being aggressive in business.
    **c.** Managing your money.

**7.** Hedonistic adaptation is simply

    **a.** The more you have, the more you want.
    **b.** The more you want, the more you have.
    **c.** Being happy with less.

**8.** People are generally happier with work if they have

    **a.** Little stress.
    **b.** Moderate stress with control over the outcomes.
    **c.** A set routine to follow.

**9.** The most important difference between a goal and a fantasy is

    **a.** Imagination.
    **b.** Procrastination.
    **c.** Action.

**10.** An A priority is

    **a.** Related to your lifetime goals.
    **b.** Something important.
    **c.** Something you have to do.

**How did you do on the quiz? Check your answers: 1. b, 2. a, 3. c, 4. b, 5. b, 6. c, 7. a, 8. b, 9. c, 10. a**

# Keys to Success
## You Are What You Think

*"Whether you think you can, or think you can't. . . you're right.*

HENRY FORD

    Our thoughts have a big impact on success in college, in our careers, and in our personal lives. Sometimes students enter college with the fear of failure. This belief can lead to anxiety and behavior that leads to failure. If you have doubts about your ability to succeed in college, you might not go to class or attempt the challenging work required in college. Unfortunately, failure in college can lead to a loss of confidence and lack of success in other areas of life as well.

    If you have doubts about finding your ideal career, you might not take the steps needed to prepare for it or find it. It is difficult to make the effort if you cannot see positive results ahead.

Beliefs influence career satisfaction. If you can find purpose and meaning in your job, you are likely to be more satisfied with it. Your beliefs can determine whether you consider your job as drudgery or fulfilling your life purpose.

Henry Ford said, "what we believe is true, comes true. What we believe is possible, becomes possible." If you believe that you will succeed, you will be more likely to take actions that lead to your success. Once you have experienced some small part of success, you will have confidence in your abilities and will continue on the road to success. Success leads to more success. It becomes a habit. You will be motivated to make the effort necessary to accomplish your goals. You might even become excited and energized along the way. You will use your gifts and talents to reach your

potential and achieve happiness. It all begins with the thoughts you choose.

> Watch your thoughts; they become words.
> Watch your words; they become actions.
> Watch your actions; they become habits.
> Watch your habits; they become character.
> Watch your character; it becomes your destiny.[15]
>
> —Frank Outlaw

To help you choose positive beliefs, picture in your mind how you want your life to be. Imagine it is here now. See all the details and experience the feelings associated with this picture. Pretend it is true until you believe it. Then take action to make your dreams come true.

## JOURNAL ENTRIES
## CREATE YOUR SUCCESS

Go to https://www.collegesuccess1.com/JournalEntries.htm for Word files of the Journal Entries.

## SUCCESS
## over the Internet

**Visit the *College Success Website* at http://www.collegesuccess1.com/**

The College Success Website is continually updated with new topics and links to the material presented in this chapter. Topics include:

- Mindset
- Grit
- Career Satisfaction
- Goal Setting

# Notes

1. "Why we have Such a Love-Hate Relationship with Work," From the Conversation, May 2, 2017, Retrieved from https://theconversation.com/why-we-have-such-a-love-hate-relationship-with-work-73027. Accessed on August 2017.

2. "To Find Work You Love, Don't (Always) Follow Your Passion," updated May 2016. Retrieved from https://80000hours.org/articles/dont-follow-your-passion/. Accessed on August 2017.

3. Kerry Hannon, *Love Your Job, the New Rules for Career Happiness* (New Jersey: John Wiley & Sons, 2015).

4. Ashley Redmond, "6 Life Hacks from Warren Buffett," *The San Diego Union Tribune,* Friday, August 4, 2017.

5. Adam Davis, "Warren Buffett's 10 Inspiring Tips for Young People." Retrieved from http://www.lifehack.org/290599/warren-buffetts-10-inspiring-tips-for-young-people. Accessed on August 29, 2017.

6. "What Makes us Happy at Work?" Research is summarized by the University of Kent. Retrieved from https://www.kent.ac.uk/careers/Choosing/career-satisfaction.htm. Accessed on August 30, 2017.

7. Martin Seligman, *Authentic Happiness* (New York: The Free Press, 2002), 48.

8. "What makes us happy at work?" Research is summarized by the University of Kent, at Retrieved from https://www.kent.ac.uk/careers/Choosing/career-satisfaction.htm., accessed on August 30, 2017.

9. Martin Seligman, *Flourish, A Visionary New Understanding of Happiness and Well-being* (New York: Simon and Schuster, 2011), 24.

10. Roman Duda, "Job Satisfaction Research," updated March 2016. Retrieved from https://80000hours.org/articles/job-satisfaction-research. Accessed on August 2017.

11. Ibid.

12. "More than job satisfaction," The American Psychological Association, December 2013, Retrieved from http://www.apa.org/monitor/2013/12/job-satisfaction.aspx. Accessed on August 2017.

13. "Top 10 Employee Performance Goal Examples for 2020." PeopleGoal, October, 16, 2019, https://www.peoplegoal.com/blog/top-10-employee-performance-goal-examples-for-2020.

14. Steven K. Scott, *A Millionaire's* Notebook, quoted in Rob Gilbert, Editor, *Bits & Pieces* (Fairfield, NJ: The Economics Press, November 4, 1999), 15.

15. Rob Gilbert, ed., Bits and Pieces (Fairfield, NJ: The Economics Press, 1998), Vol. R, No. 40, p. 7.

# CHECKLIST FOR A SATISFYING CAREER

Read each statement and think about your current career choice or the options you are considering. Place a checkmark next to the items that are true about your career choice. Before you begin, you may want to review the self-assessment exercises that you have completed in this book, and as part of this course.

My career choice (or tentative career choice) is _____

1. _____ My career matches my personality type.

2. _____ This career matches my interests. I would enjoy doing this type of work.

3. _____ This career will allow me to live the lifestyle that I want.

4. _____ This career matches my values (what I think is important).

5. _____ I have the skills necessary to be successful in this career or I am willing to obtain these skills.

6. _____ This career provides the kind of salary I need to live the way I want.

7. _____ This career has a positive outlook for the future. The career will exist in the future and there will likely be job openings in this area.

8. _____ I am willing to complete the education or training required to enter this career.

9. _____ This career choice will help me to accomplish my lifetime goals.

10. _____ This career provides the opportunity to help others or contribute to the greater good.

11. _____ It is likely that I would enjoy working with others in this career. I can work with people who have goals and interests that match my own.

12. _____ This career provides the opportunities to pursue my hobbies and interests either as part of the job or outside the job.

13. _____ This career provides the opportunity to maintain my own mental and physical health. It provides time for relaxation and recreation

14. _____ This career allows time to spend with the people who are important in my life.

Look at the items above fill in the following chart.

| Positive Aspects of This Career | Negative Aspects of This Career |
| --- | --- |
| | |

How would this career be a good match for you? Are there any negative aspects that you would have to overcome?

# MY LIFETIME GOALS: BRAINSTORMING ACTIVITY

1. Think about the goals that you would like to accomplish in your life. At the end of your life, you do not want to say, "I wish I would have _____." Set a timer for five minutes and write whatever comes to mind about what you would like to do and accomplish over your lifetime. Include goals in these areas: career, personal relationships, travel, and financial security, or any area that is important to you. Write down all your ideas. The goal is to generate as many ideas as possible in five minutes. You can reflect on which ones are most important later. You may want to do this as part of a group activity in your class.

Look over the ideas you wrote above and highlight or underline the goals that are most important to you.

2. Ask yourself what you would like to accomplish in the next five years. Think about where you want to be in college, what you want to do in your career, and what you want to do in your personal life. Set a timer and write whatever comes to mind in five minutes. The goal is to write down as many ideas as possible.

Again, look over the ideas you wrote and highlight or underline the ideas that are most important to you.

3. What goals would you like to accomplish in the next year? What are some steps that you can begin now to accomplish your lifetime goals? Consider work, study, leisure, and social goals. Set your timer for five minutes and write down your goals for the next year.

Review what you wrote and highlight or underline the ideas that are most important to you. When writing your goals, include fun activities as well as taking care of others.

Looking at the items that you have highlighted or underlined, make a list of your lifetime goals using the form that follows. Make sure your goals are specific enough so that you can break them into steps you can achieve.

# MY LIFETIME GOALS

Using the ideas that you brainstormed in the previous exercise, make a list of your lifetime goals. Make sure your goals are specific and concrete. Begin with goals that you would like to accomplish over a lifetime. In the second section, think about the goals you can accomplish over the next one to three years.

Long-Term Goals (lifetime goals)

Short-Term Goals (one to three years)

What are some steps you can take now to accomplish intermediate and long-term goals?

# SUCCESSFUL GOAL SETTING

Look at your list of lifetime goals. Which one is most important? Write the goal here:




Answer these questions about the goal you have listed above.

1. What skills, abilities, and resources do you have to achieve this goal? What skills, abilities, and resources will you need to develop to achieve this goal?




2. Do you believe you can achieve it? Write a brief positive statement about achieving this goal.




3. State your goal in specific terms that can be observed or counted. Rewrite your goal if necessary.




4. Write a brief statement about how this goal will give you personal satisfaction.




5. How will you motivate yourself to achieve this goal?

6. What are your personal values that match this goal?

7. List some steps that you will take to accomplish this goal.

8. When will you finish this goal?

9. What roadblocks will make this goal difficult to achieve?

10. How will you deal with these roadblocks?

# POST ASSESSMENT

Now that you have finished the text, complete the following assessment to measure your improvement. Compare your results to the assessment taken at the beginning of the course.

## Measure Your Success

The following statements represent major topics included in the textbook. Read the following statements and rate how true they are for you at the present time. At the end of the course, you will have the opportunity to complete this assessment again to measure your progress.

5    Definitely true
4    Mostly true
3    Somewhat true
2    Seldom true
1    Never true

_____ I understand the steps in choosing a major and career.

_____ I understand how education will affect my future earnings.

_____ I know how to use motivation techniques to be successful.

_____ I have control over my life and can create my future.

_____ I usually practice positive thinking.

_____ I have a visual picture of my future success.

_____ I have a clear idea of what happiness means to me.

_____ Total points for Creating Success

_____ I can describe my personality type.

_____ I can list careers that match my personality type.

_____ I can describe my personal strengths and talents based on my personality type.

_____ I understand how my personality type affects how I manage my time and money.

_____ I know what college majors are most in demand.

_____ I am confident that I have chosen the best major for myself.

_____ Courses related to my major are interesting and exciting to me.

_____ Total points for Personality and Major

_____ I can describe my vocational interests.

_____ I can list careers that match my vocational interests.

_____ I can list my top five values.

_____ I generally consider my most important values when making decisions.

_____ My actions are generally guided by my personal values.

_____ My personal values motivate me to be successful.

_____ I can balance work, study, and leisure activities.

_____ Total points for Interests and Values

_____ I understand how my mindset affects my intelligences.

_____ I understand how grit and perseverance affect my intelligences.

_____ I understand the concept of multiple intelligences.

_____ I can list my multiple intelligences.

_____ I can list the careers that match my intelligences.

_____ I am aware of my emotional intelligence and use it to create positive relationships.

_____ I believe that I can create my own future.

_____ Total points for Multiple Intelligences

_____ I understand how current employment trends will affect my future.

_____ I can list my highest job skills and those that need improvement.

_____ I know how to do career research.

_____ I am aware of the job outlook for careers in which I am interested.

_____ I have an educational plan that matches my academic and career goals.

_____ I know the steps in making a good career decision.

_____ I know how to match my career to my personality, interests, values, intelligences, and skills.

_____ Total points for Career and Education

_____ I know how to increase my chances for employment while in college.

_____ I know how to write a good resume and cover letter.

_____ I understand personal branding and know how to market myself online.

_____ I know how to use social media to find a job.

_____ I am familiar with online tools for job search.

_____ I know how to interview for a job.

_____ I know about options for creating my own business.

_____ Total points for Job Search Strategies

_____ I know how to find passion and meaning in my work.

_____ I understand the role of money in my own career satisfaction.

_____ I know about the predictors of job satisfaction.

_____ I can identify what makes people happy at work.

_____ I know how to be successful on the job.

_____ I have some specific and achievable goals for the future.

_____ I use priorities in managing my time to accomplish my future goals.

_____ Total Points for Career Satisfaction

Total Your Points

_____ Creating Success

_____ Personality and Major

_____ Interests and Values

_____ Multiple Intelligences and Goal Setting

_____ Career and Education

_____ Job Search Strategies

_____ Grand total points

If you scored

221–245    You have excellent skills for creating your future career, but you can always learn something new.

220–197    You have good skills for creating your future career, but could improve.

196–173    You have average skills for creating your future career.

Below 172  Review some of the materials in this textbook to increase the skills for creating your future career.

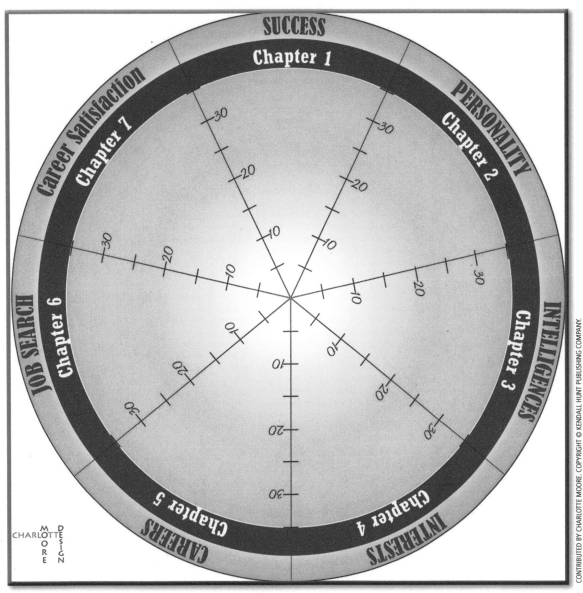

Compare your results to those on this same assessment in Chapter 1. How much did you improve?

# COURSE EVALUATION

1. What did you think of this course?

_____ A. This was one of the best courses I ever had.

_____ B. This course was excellent.

_____ C. This course was very good.

_____ D. This course was satisfactory.

_____ E. This course was not satisfactory.

2. How helpful was this course in choosing a major or career or confirming you choice of a major or career?

_____ A. Extremely helpful

_____ B. Very helpful

_____ C. Helpful

_____ D. Not helpful

_____ E. Unknown

3. How helpful was this course in improving your chances for success in college?

_____ A. Extremely helpful

_____ B. Very helpful

_____ C. Helpful

_____ D. Not helpful

_____ E. Unknown

4. How helpful was this course in improving your chances for success in your future career?

_____ A. Extremely helpful

_____ B. Very helpful

_____ C. Helpful

_____ D. Not helpful

_____ E. Unknown

5. How helpful was this course in building your self-confidence?

_____ A. Extremely helpful

_____ B. Very helpful

_____ C. Helpful

_____ D. Not helpful

_____ E. Unknown

6. Please rate the textbook used for this class.

_____ A.  Outstanding

_____ B.  Excellent

_____ C.  Satisfactory

_____ D.  Needs improvement

7. Please rate the instructor in this class.

_____ A.  Outstanding

_____ B.  Excellent

_____ C.  Satisfactory

_____ D.  Needs improvement

8. Would you recommend this course to a friend?

_____ A.  Yes

_____ B.  No

9. Do you plan to continue your college studies next semester?

_____ A.  Yes

_____ B.  No

10. Please tell what you liked about this class and how it was useful to you.

11. Do you have any suggestions for improving the class or text?

# INDEX